EYEWITNESS
REPTILE

Madagascan chameleon

Soft-shelled turtle

Jackson's
chameleon

Indian python

Starred tortoise

Radiated tortoise

EYEWITNESS
REPTILE

Written by
COLIN McCARTHY

Sinaloan milk snake

Basilisk lizard

Red-eared terrapin

Caiman

Eyed lizard

DK

Tree skink

Tegu lizard

Caiman

Grass snake

Flying snake

Alligator snapping turtle

Corn snake

DK | Penguin Random House

Project editors Gillian Denton, Lynne Williams
Art editor Neville Graham
Senior editor Helen Parker
Senior art editors Jacquie Gulliver, Julia Harris
Production Louise Barratt
Picture research Kathy Lockley
Special photography Karl Shone, Jane Burton,
Kim Taylor, Colin Keates

SECOND EDITION
Revised by David Burnie

RELAUNCH EDITION

DK DELHI
Project Editor Priyanka Kharbanda
Project Art Editor Neha Sharma
Assistant Editor Antara Raghavan
Assistant Art Editor Priyanka Bansal
DTP Designer Pawan Kumar
Picture Researcher Sakshi Saluja
Jacket Designer Juhi Sheth

DK LONDON
Senior Art Editor Spencer Holbrook
Editor Anna Streiffert Limerick US Senior Editor Margaret Parrish
US Editor Jill Hamilton Jacket Editor Claire Gell
Jacket Design Development Manager Sophia MTT
Producer, pre-production Jacqueline Street Producer Gary Batchelor
Managing Editor Francesca Baines Managing Art Editor Philip Letsu
Publisher Andrew Macintyre Associate Publishing Director Liz Wheeler
Art Director Karen Self Design Director Philip Ormerod
Publishing Director Jonathan Metcalf

This Eyewitness ® Guide has been conceived by Dorling Kindersley Limited and Editions Gallimard

This American Edition, 2017
First American Edition, 1991
Published in the United States by DK Publishing
1450 Broadway, Suite 801, New York, NY 10018

Published in Great Britain by Dorling Kindersley Limited

A catalog record for this book is available from the Library of Congress.
ISBN 978-1-4654-6249-7 (Paperback)
ISBN 978-1-4654-6252-7 (ALB)

DK books are available at special discounts when purchased in bulk for sales
promotions, premiums, fund-raising, or educational use. For details, contact:
DK Publishing, Special Markets, 1450 Broadway, Suite 801, New York, NY 10018
SpecialSales@dk.com

Printed and bound in China

A WORLD OF IDEAS:
SEE ALL THERE IS TO KNOW

www.dk.com

Contents

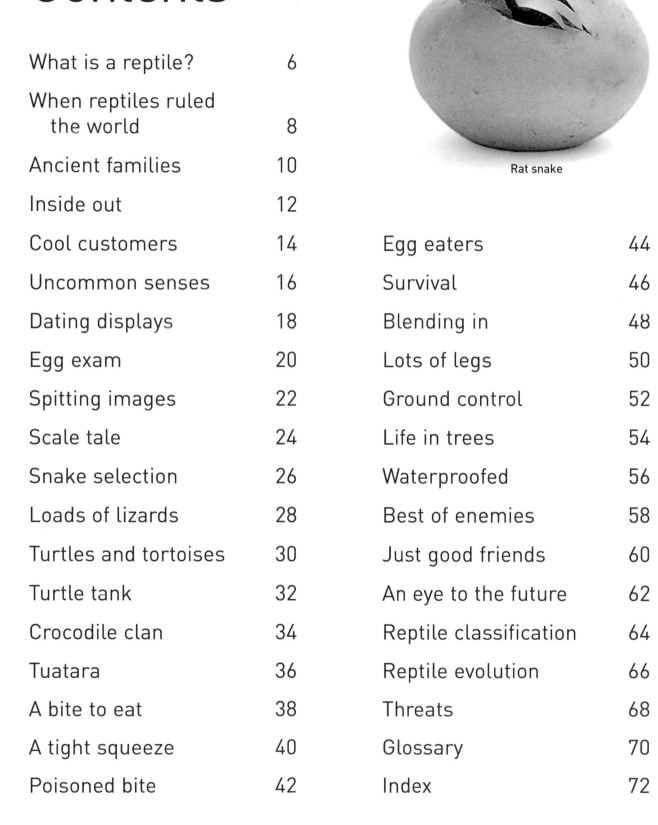

Rat snake

What is a reptile?

Four groups of reptiles exist today: snakes and lizards, the crocodile family, turtles and tortoises, and the tuatara. Like fish, birds, mammals, and amphibians, reptiles are vertebrates (have backbones). Reptile young are usually born on land, looking like miniature adults. Scaly skin keeps in moisture, helping them live in dry places, but allows body heat to escape; therefore, they rely on heat from the outside environment—they are "cold-blooded."

Scaly skin

Extra-long toe for added support

Dream dragons

Reptiles have been featured in mythology for hundreds of years. Dragons were described by famous Italian explorer Marco Polo, who may have seen huge lizard and snake species, and flying lizards, on his travels in the East. Multi-headed hydra was a beast of Greek mythology who grew two heads when one was cut off. Legend says that Hercules killed it by sealing each neck as a head was cut off.

Hydra

What is not a reptile?

Salamanders look like lizards, but they are amphibians, not reptiles. Amphibians are often mistaken for reptiles, even though they are very different: amphibians have no scales because they breathe through their skin, and most breed near water before laying eggs in the water. The European fire salamander (above), however, keeps her eggs in her body until they hatch, and gives birth to tadpoles in shallow water.

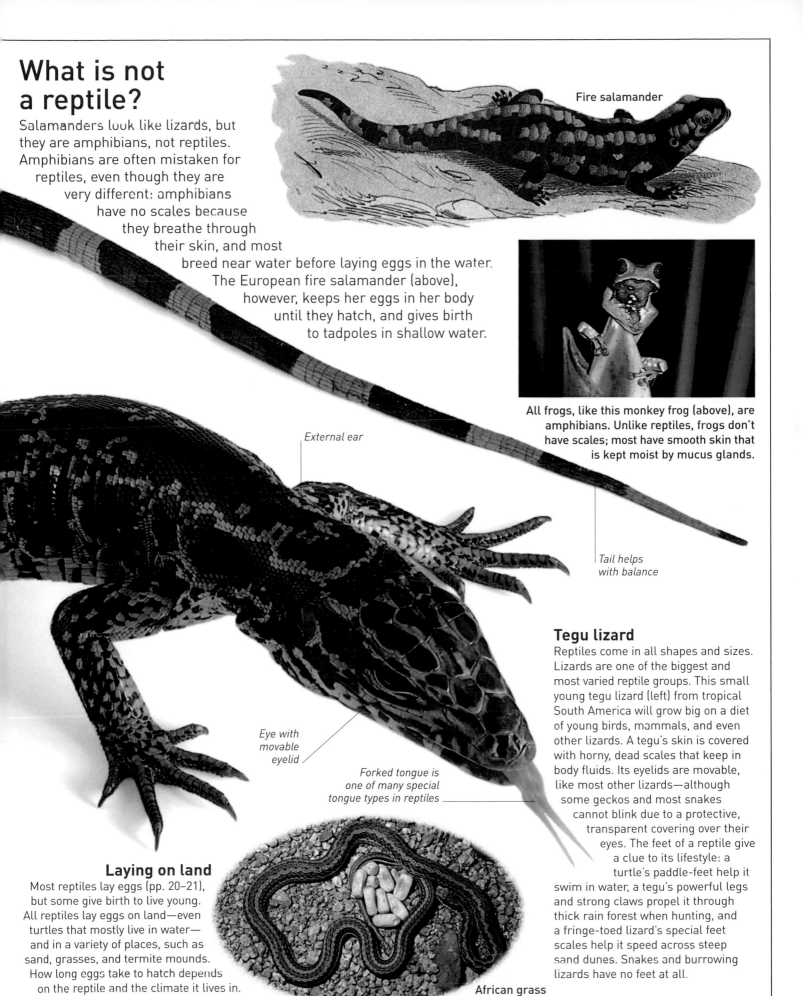

Fire salamander

All frogs, like this monkey frog (above), are amphibians. Unlike reptiles, frogs don't have scales; most have smooth skin that is kept moist by mucus glands.

External ear

Tail helps
with balance

Eye with
movable
eyelid

Forked tongue is
one of many special
tongue types in reptiles

Tegu lizard

Reptiles come in all shapes and sizes. Lizards are one of the biggest and most varied reptile groups. This small young tegu lizard (left) from tropical South America will grow big on a diet of young birds, mammals, and even other lizards. A tegu's skin is covered with horny, dead scales that keep in body fluids. Its eyelids are movable, like most other lizards—although some geckos and most snakes cannot blink due to a protective, transparent covering over their eyes. The feet of a reptile give a clue to its lifestyle: a turtle's paddle-feet help it swim in water, a tegu's powerful legs and strong claws propel it through thick rain forest when hunting, and a fringe-toed lizard's special feet scales help it speed across steep sand dunes. Snakes and burrowing lizards have no feet at all.

Laying on land

Most reptiles lay eggs (pp. 20–21), but some give birth to live young. All reptiles lay eggs on land—even turtles that mostly live in water—and in a variety of places, such as sand, grasses, and termite mounds. How long eggs take to hatch depends on the reptile and the climate it lives in.

African grass
snake with eggs

When reptiles ruled the world

Pterosaurs
These flying reptiles ruled the air for more than 100 million years, until they became extinct. Their wings were made of a membrane stretched between a long finger and leg.

The first reptiles evolved from amphibians more than 300 million years ago (MYA)—in the Carboniferous (Pennsylvanian and Mississippian) Period. But it was not until the Mesozoic era, 251 to 65 MYA, that reptiles ruled life on Earth: dinosaurs dominated the land; other reptiles ruled the skies and seas. It is mainly thanks to their eggs—which, unlike those of amphibians, have shells and so can be laid on dry land—that reptiles have spread across the world.

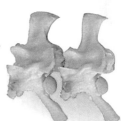

Vertebrae of *Palaeophis,* an ancient sea snake

Ancient giants
The enormous vertebrae (spinal bones, above) of extinct sea snake *Palaeophis*, found in West Africa, proved that a snake four times larger than a modern python lived in the Cenozoic era. These vertebrae (right) are from a present-day 2-ft (6-m)-long python.

Vertebrae of a modern python

TIME CHART OF THE EARTH					
Paleozoic era		Mesozoic era			Cenozoic era
Carboniferous Period	Permian Period	Triassic Period	Jurassic Period	Cretaceous Period	Palaeocene Epoch to the present day
359 MYA	299 MYA	251 MYA	202 MYA	145 MYA	65 MYA
		Turtles, tortoises, and terrapins			
		Crocodilians			
		Lizards			
				Snakes	

Duration of each period not to scale

Slow to change
Lizards first appeared about 200 MYA, evolving alongside dinosaurs. Lizard fossils are rare, but there is evidence (such as below) that different lizards, with a body that is typical of lizards today, existed at the end of the Mesozoic era.

Pointed teeth for piercing and eating fish

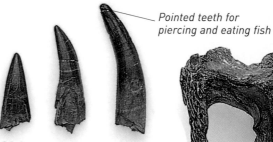

Old crocs
Crocodiles are as old as dinosaurs, first evolving in the Triassic Period. The crocodile skull (right) has hardly changed over time, but the long, sharp, pointed teeth (above) of early crocs are more like those of pure fish-eaters—different from the spikelike teeth of modern crocs who eat fish, land animals, and the occasional plant.

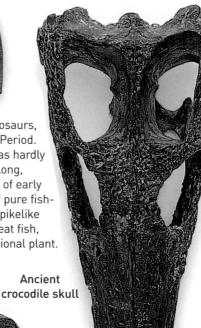

Ancient crocodile skull

Dog jaw

This skull (below), with its doglike jaws, is from the meat-eating reptile *Cynognathus*—an advanced form of the mammal-like reptiles that dominated the land during the Permian and Triassic periods (299–202 MYA). Mammals evolved from this group of reptiles about 195 MYA.

Skull of *Cynognathus*

Strong jaw and large teeth for eating meat

A reconstruction of an advanced, mammal-like reptile showing an improved, nonsprawling posture

Turtles first

Turtles are the oldest living reptile group, with fossils dating back 220 million years. Turtles survived many environmental changes, and produced many land and marine forms. Some living species are as small as a tennis ball, but prehistoric turtles could be as big as a car.

Toothless

A modern turtle skull is unique from other vertebrate skulls because it has no openings in the bone for jaw muscles to attach, and no teeth. The skull of late Triassic turtle *Proganochelys* (right) shows that modern and ancient turtle skulls are similar, except for evidence of teeth in the old turtle's jaw.

Fossilized *Proganochelys* skull

Fossilized remains of an ancient turtle

Ancient families

Animals are classified according to how they evolved. In the same way that cousins are related because they share the same grandparents, animals with shared ancestors are grouped together. Lizards and snakes are closely related, but crocodiles actually share more ancestry with birds than other reptiles. However, a lack of evidence about ancestors means that groupings are also based on shared features.

Reptiles today

Only four groups of the many prehistoric reptiles are still alive today. The largest group is lizards and snakes. The smaller groups used to be bigger—there used to be 108 species of crocodilians; today, there are just 23.

	Lizards 5,500 species
	Snakes 3,400 species
	Turtles 317 species
	Crocodilians 23 species
	Tuatara 2 species

Number of reptile species alive today

Monitor lizard

Lizards

Within each reptile group, some species are more closely related than others. Iguanas, agamas, and chameleons are closely related and, with geckos, form the most primitive (least evolved) lizard group. Monitors, beaded lizards, and glass lizards are also grouped together.

Dwarf gecko

David and Goliath

The world's largest reptile is the estuarine, or saltwater, crocodile, found from southern India to northern Australia. It usually grows to a length of 16 ft (5 m), but some 26-ft (8-m)-long crocs have been recorded. The world's smallest reptiles are dwarf geckos from the Caribbean islands, which can be just 0.6 in (16 mm) long.

Estuarine crocodile

Snakes

Legless reptiles with long, slender bodies, snakes are split into three groups: primitive snakes (such as pythons and boas), blind snakes (such as thread snakes), and advanced snakes (such as cobras, sea snakes, and vipers). Snakes are found all over the world, except in very cold areas.

Indian python

Turtles

Turtles have short, broad bodies that are enclosed in a bony shell, usually covered by horny plates; sometimes, they have leathery skin. They live on land and in water, and are divided into two groups, based on how the neck bends as it retreats into the shell: hidden-neck turtles (such as terrapins and tortoises) and side-necked turtles (such as snake-necked turtles and African mud turtles).

Hermann's tortoise

Crocodilians

This very old group of reptiles is divided into three families—crocodiles, gharials, and alligators (which includes caimans). Crocodilians are, in many ways, a more advanced group than other reptiles: their blood circulation system is more efficient, they are thought to have a more intelligent brain, and they show greater care for their young.

Caiman

Inside out

The bones of many reptiles keep growing throughout their lives, causing some, such as pythons, crocodiles, and giant tortoises, to grow to gigantic sizes. While mammals lose their teeth when they are old, most reptiles do not, but instead continue to shed and grow new ones.

Tail vertebra

Trunk vertebra

The insides of a lizard are symmetrical, unlike a snake's.

Chameleon skeleton

Skull

Ribs

Chameleons

Like many lizards, the chameleon has a highly specialized skeleton. Adapted for life in trees and bushes, its broad body provides stability when its weight is centered on narrow twigs; its fingers and toes are good at grasping; and its tail is prehensile, wrapping around twigs with a tight grip.

Caiman skeleton

Skull

Neck vertebra

Caimans

A long skull with high-set eyes and nostrils allows a caiman to float with just its nose and eyes above the water. It has two pairs of short legs on its long body, with partly webbed toes—five on the front feet, four on the back. Like all crocodilians, its upper jaw is almost solid bone.

Ribs

Three outside toes and two inside toes on each foot help grip branches

Tail vertebra

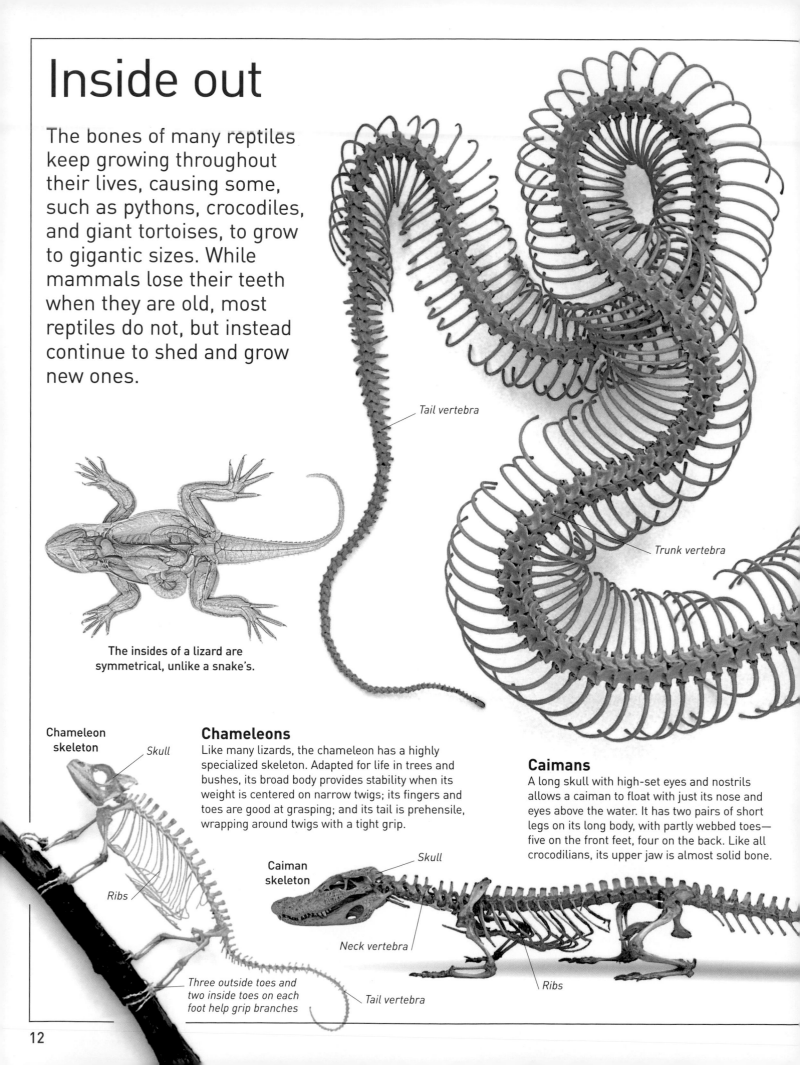

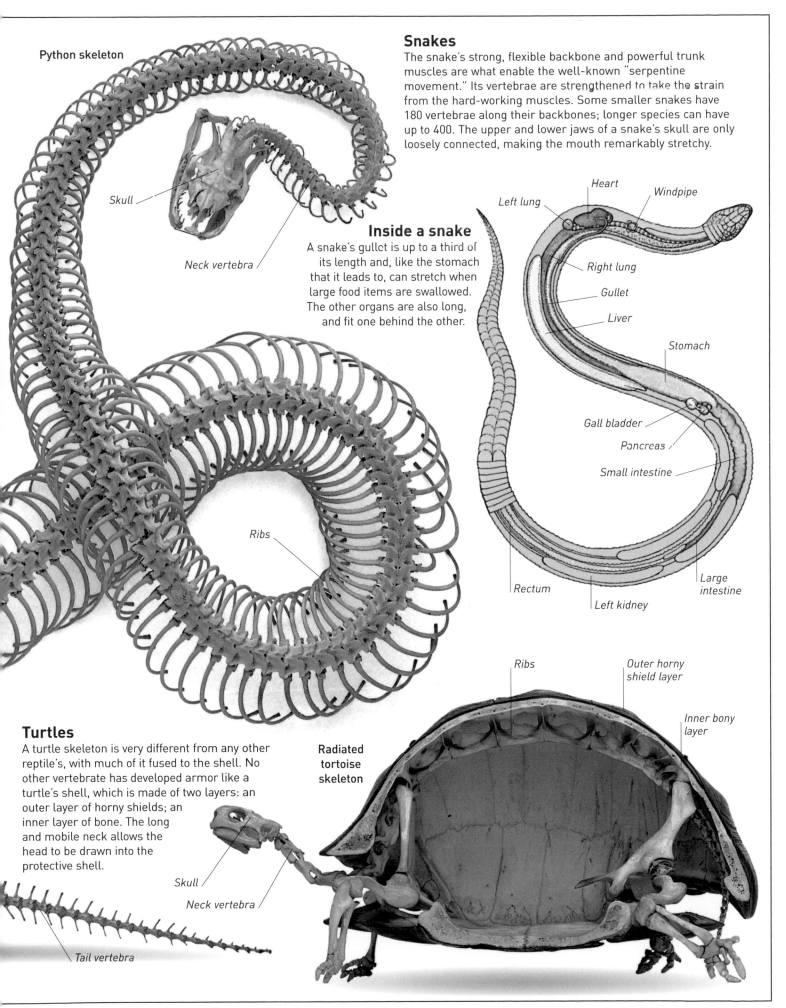

Python skeleton

Skull

Neck vertebra

Ribs

Snakes

The snake's strong, flexible backbone and powerful trunk muscles are what enable the well-known "serpentine movement." Its vertebrae are strengthened to take the strain from the hard-working muscles. Some smaller snakes have 180 vertebrae along their backbones; longer species can have up to 400. The upper and lower jaws of a snake's skull are only loosely connected, making the mouth remarkably stretchy.

Inside a snake

A snake's gullet is up to a third of its length and, like the stomach that it leads to, can stretch when large food items are swallowed. The other organs are also long, and fit one behind the other.

Heart

Left lung

Windpipe

Right lung

Gullet

Liver

Stomach

Gall bladder

Pancreas

Small intestine

Rectum

Left kidney

Large intestine

Ribs

Outer horny shield layer

Inner bony layer

Turtles

A turtle skeleton is very different from any other reptile's, with much of it fused to the shell. No other vertebrate has developed armor like a turtle's shell, which is made of two layers: an outer layer of horny shields; an inner layer of bone. The long and mobile neck allows the head to be drawn into the protective shell.

Radiated tortoise skeleton

Skull

Neck vertebra

Tail vertebra

Cool customers

Reptiles are cold-blooded (pp. 6–7)—their body temperature changes with that of their surroundings. To be active and able to function, they must be warm—in fact, high temperatures are needed for them to digest food—so they thrive in hot climates. On chilly mornings, reptiles bask in sunshine to warm up; when the day gets hot, they move into the shade to cool down. By moving in and out of the sun, their internal temperature stays constant. Low temperatures in poor weather make reptiles slow, and in danger from predators.

Lizard basking in the sunshine

Taking it easy
Crocodiles cool down by opening their mouths to let moisture evaporate, or by lying in cool water. American crocodiles lie in burrows when temperatures are too hot.

Keeping cool
In the early morning, this agama lizard (above) sits in the sun. Once warm, it runs after insects to eat. When the day gets hot, it cools down in the shade. This pattern of warming and cooling varies with the seasons: in cool months, reptiles are only active at midday, when it is warm; in summer months, they may go underground at midday to avoid overheating.

Sand lizard

Boiling over
Some people go red with anger as blood rushes to their face, making them look hot—but their blood temperature does not actually rise.

Ground gecko

Taking cover

Like many other desert snakes, the sand viper avoids the heat of the day; it is mainly nocturnal, and sinks itself in the sand if caught in hot sun. It moves in a "sidewinding" fashion (p. 53), and may travel up to 0.6 miles (1 km) while hunting for small mammals and lizards.

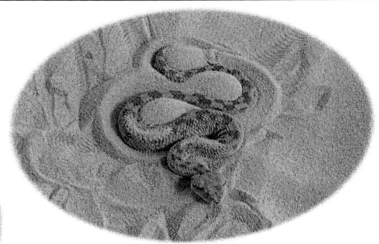

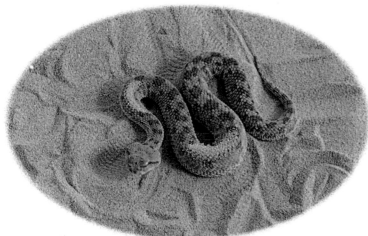

1 Going...
A sand viper retreats into the sand, tail first, wriggling as it goes. Its eyes are well protected from irritating grains of sand by the transparent covering that shields them.

2 Going...
Shuffling and rocking, the snake descends vertically, shoveling sand up and over its back. Its scales help work the grains of sand along its body to cover it.

3 Gone!
The sand viper is almost completely buried. Soon, only the top of its head will be visible. Bedding down in the hot desert sand protects it from the scorching sun, and also makes a perfect hiding place when either enemies or prey are nearby.

Snake leaves visible marks as it moves in the sand

Uncommon senses

Reptiles, like all vertebrates, use smell, sight, and hearing to find out about their surroundings—and some reptiles have additional "senses." Snakes and some lizards "smell" using their tongue and special sensory cells (Jacobson's organ). Some snakes are sensitive to infrared heat, which means they can detect warm-blooded prey in the dark. In some reptiles, however, the common senses are underdeveloped; burrowing reptiles have poor eyesight, and snakes cannot hear very well.

Alligator roar
Alligators communicate over vast distances by bellowing. The sound can be very loud—up to 92 decibels at 16 ft (5 m), which is roughly as loud as the propeller engine of a small airplane.

Swiveling eye is set on a turret

Eyelids can close to tiny peepholes

Special toes grasp branches like pincers

Broad horizons
The chameleon has an amazingly wide field of vision, and can move each eye independently of the other. If it sees a fly, it can keep one eye pointed at the fly while the other eye scans the area for enemies, at the same time maneuvering itself toward the fly for capture. When it is close, the chameleon swivels both eyes toward the fly to see it with a binocular vision similar to that of humans. With both eyes fixed on the fly, the chameleon can better judge its position and aim.

Small but noisy
Most geckos have a voice; some chirp and click, usually when mating or defending territory. When distressed, some produce ultrasounds, which can only be heard by mammals or birds—predators the gecko wishes to alarm.

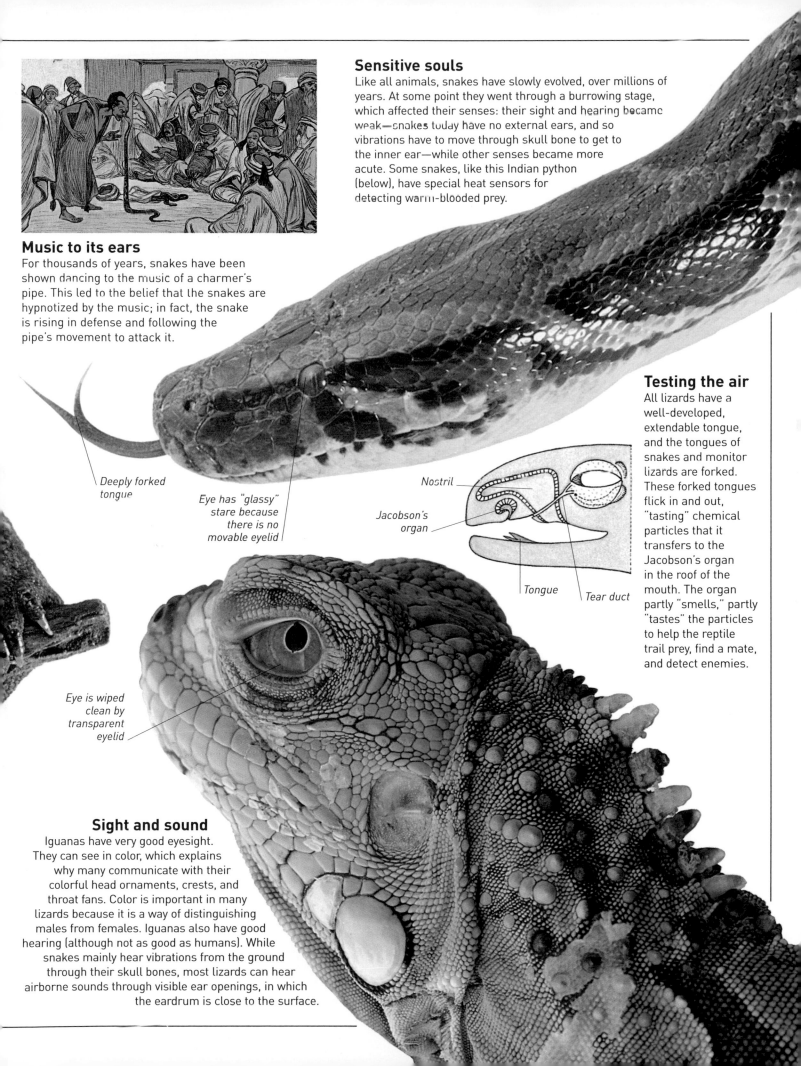

Sensitive souls

Like all animals, snakes have slowly evolved, over millions of years. At some point they went through a burrowing stage, which affected their senses: their sight and hearing became weak—snakes today have no external ears, and so vibrations have to move through skull bone to get to the inner ear—while other senses became more acute. Some snakes, like this Indian python (below), have special heat sensors for detecting warm-blooded prey.

Music to its ears

For thousands of years, snakes have been shown dancing to the music of a charmer's pipe. This led to the belief that the snakes are hypnotized by the music; in fact, the snake is rising in defense and following the pipe's movement to attack it.

Deeply forked tongue

Eye has "glassy" stare because there is no movable eyelid

Testing the air

All lizards have a well-developed, extendable tongue, and the tongues of snakes and monitor lizards are forked. These forked tongues flick in and out, "tasting" chemical particles that it transfers to the Jacobson's organ in the roof of the mouth. The organ partly "smells," partly "tastes" the particles to help the reptile trail prey, find a mate, and detect enemies.

Nostril

Jacobson's organ

Tongue

Tear duct

Eye is wiped clean by transparent eyelid

Sight and sound

Iguanas have very good eyesight. They can see in color, which explains why many communicate with their colorful head ornaments, crests, and throat fans. Color is important in many lizards because it is a way of distinguishing males from females. Iguanas also have good hearing (although not as good as humans). While snakes mainly hear vibrations from the ground through their skull bones, most lizards can hear airborne sounds through visible ear openings, in which the eardrum is close to the surface.

Dating displays

Reptiles spend most of their days adjusting their body temperature, searching for food, and escaping from predators. But, in mating season, they also need to attract a mate in order to reproduce. Male lizards often display bright colors to appeal to females, and some also show off with elaborate frills and crests. These same displays are also used to warn off male rivals.

Birth control
Many snakes can store sperm, in some cases for months, after they have mated. This means that, when there is lots of food to feed the young, and conditions are favorable, the snakes can use the stored sperm to fertilize more eggs to produce more young.

Flashy
The male frigatebird (right) and the anole lizard (above) both attract mates by inflating their pouch.

A couple of swells
Anole lizards are highly territorial. The males inflate their brilliant-reddish throat sacs as a sign of aggression toward other males. Two same-sized lizards may flaunt their throat sacs at one another for hours at a time, while a smaller lizard would instantly retreat. There are many different species of anole lizard, which live in the tropical areas of South and Central America. They are sometimes called "American chameleons"—although they are really iguanas—due to their ability to change from green to different shades of brown. This helps them blend well into the green and brown vegetation they live in, protecting them from enemies.

Spring mates
Giant tortoises mate in the spring. The male will often show interest by ramming the female in the side with his shell. The act of mating can take several hours.

Snake charmers
Once a male snake has found a female, he stimulates her into mating by rubbing his chin along her back, while their bodies and tails intertwine. During the mating season, two male snakes will sometimes perform a kind of combat dance, as they vie for a favored female. Reptiles often avoid fighting (during which one or both snakes may be injured) by signaling their intentions from a distance, proving which creature is superior without having to fight.

Test of strength
Male monitor lizards (right) rear up and wrestle at the start of the mating season. The weaker animal usually gives up before it is injured.

Tails intertwine during mating

Throat sac is inflated to attract a female or as a sign of aggression

Egg exam

Most young reptiles develop inside an egg, cushioned in a bag of fluid called the amnion. Most reptile eggs have a soft, flexible shell, although some have hard shells. Oxygen and moisture is passed to the young through the shell, and the yolk provides it with food.

Snakes

Most snake eggs have parchmentlike shells. The young hatch by using a special, sharp egg tooth to break the shell. Most snakes bury their eggs. However, some are viviparous—they give birth to live young, not eggs.

Ground python egg

Indian python egg

Underground

This strange-looking egg (left) was laid by a ground python, a burrowing snake from West Africa. The egg is large in proportion to the mother; a 33-in (85-cm)-long female may lay eggs 4 in (12 cm) in length.

Mother love

The female Indian python coils around her 30 or so leathery-shelled eggs (above), and twitches her muscles to warm the eggs.

Common as muck

The common African house snake often lays eight to 10 eggs in manure heaps or termite mounds.

African house snake egg

Fact or fiction?

In Greek mythology, a female tribe, the Amazons, hated and lived without men. Some females in the reptile world, like the whiptail (right), can reproduce without mating.

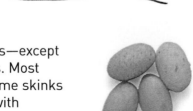

Whiptail lizard

Monitor lizard egg

Parson's chameleon eggs

Javan bloodsucker egg

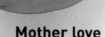

Lizards

Most lizard eggs have leathery shells—except geckos, which lay hard-shelled eggs. Most lizards ignore their laid eggs, but some skinks return to brood, warming the eggs with their bodies.

Tokay gecko eggs

Stuck on you

The tokay gecko, like many geckos and skinks, lays eggs two at a time. They are soft and sticky at first, but soon harden and stick to the surface on which they were laid.

Buried alive

While some chameleons give birth to live young, Parson's chameleon lays 30–40 eggs in a hole in the ground. It fills it in to protect its eggs, which can take up to 20 months to hatch.

Spindle eggs

The eggs of the Javan bloodsucker lizard are a peculiar spindle shape. It is not clear why; species closely related to it have normal, oval eggs.

Nest intruders

The Nile monitor lizard prefers to lay her 40–60 eggs in a termite mound. The heat inside the mound incubates the eggs.

Crocodilians

Caimans and alligators make mounds out of fresh vegetation, soil, and leaf litter for their hard-shelled eggs. Crocodiles and gharials make hole nests in exposed beaches and dry, crumbly soil. The female often stays close by to stop egg thieves from raiding the nest. All crocodilian eggs have to be kept warm; the sex of the baby hatchling is decided by temperature in early incubation.

Dwarf crocodile egg

Alligator egg

Crocodile spirit

People of Papua New Guinea have long lived alongside crocodiles, and some believe they are magical spirits. The ceremonial shield (below) shows a figure in a crocodile.

Lending a claw

The female American alligator lays 35–40 eggs in her mound nest. When they have hatched, the babies and their mother tear open the nest to let them out.

Little mystery

The African dwarf crocodile is mostly nocturnal. It lays no more than 20 eggs (above), but they are large and laid in a specially made mound.

Turtles and tortoises

Tortoises, and some turtles, lay hard-shelled eggs; marine and some river turtles lay soft. Most dig a hole for their eggs, and may return to the same spot every year. The sex can be decided by temperature in incubation.

Snake-necked turtle egg

Spur-thighed tortoise egg

Matamata egg

Matamata

The eggs of this strange South American turtle (above) look like ping-pong balls. Like all aquatic turtles, the matamata must leave the water to lay her eggs.

Spur-thighed tortoise

The spur-thighed tortoise is found in the Mediterranean. It was once exported to pet shops in northern Europe, but few survived. Importing them is now against the law in most places.

Snake-necked turtle

The Australian snake-necked turtle leaves the water at night, after rainfall, to lay eggs in a hole nest on dry land.

Galapagos tortoise egg

Gentle giant

The Galapagos giant tortoise is one of the world's biggest. It lays eggs in sun-baked soil, where they incubate for up to 200 days. Many eggs are destroyed by foraging rats and pigs, brought to the islands by humans.

Mass nesting

Every year, Olive Ridley sea turtles arrive during very high tides on tropical beaches. Each female digs a hole, lays 100 eggs, then returns to the sea.

Protective eggs

Reptilian eggs are made up of layers: a brittle outer shell—which has been broken (below) to reveal a flexible inner layer. Under this is the fluid-filled amnion, which houses the embryo. The yolk supplies the baby with food.

Shell allows embryo to breathe

Embryo

Amnion

Yolk sac

Spitting images

Baby reptiles look like miniature adults when they hatch, and can fend for themselves. This is necessary because most reptiles leave their eggs once they are laid—although some lizards and snakes do protect them, and some watch over their young. Baby reptiles are able to feed themselves and survive in the environment that they'll inhabit once they're mature. A young reptile eats smaller prey than an adult—for example, a young crocodile can survive on insects, but as it grows, it will need larger meals, including birds, fish, and mammals.

Young caiman

Like mother, like daughter
This young caiman (left) is born fully formed and able to fend for itself. Like the young alligator (above), it will stay close to its mother for a few weeks, sometimes using her as a basking platform. But, at the first sign of danger, it will dive underwater for cover.

Hatching out
Snake eggs often swell and get heavier as they absorb moisture from their surroundings. The time they take to hatch depends on temperature: the warmer it is, the faster the eggs develop. So the mother will often lay her eggs in a place that is warm and slightly moist—such as compost heaps, where rotting vegetation produces heat. Often, the baby snake is much longer than the egg it hatched from; inside the egg, its whole body was tightly coiled.

1 The egg
This is the egg of a common and large North American rat snake. Its mating season is from April to June and in the fall. Between June and August, the female lays five to 30 soft-shelled, oblong eggs.

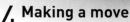

4 Making a move
When it decides to leave the egg, the snake does so quickly, and slithers along in the normal snakelike way (p.53). However, if a snake is removed from its egg a little too early, it will writhe around, unable to move properly. It therefore seems likely that the snake does not become fully coordinated until just before hatching.

Big babies
The adder, Britain's only venomous snake, produces young that are incredibly large compared to the eggs in which they develop.

Looks can deceive

Most geckos lay their eggs between pieces of bark or stick them to a wall. This sandstone gecko laid her eggs in rock crevices. Because they were exposed to the elements, the eggs had hard shells (pp.20–21). Although many geckos lay their eggs in shared sites, they do not take care of their young—it is unusual to see mother and young as close as this (right). The young are independent from birth, but are not able to reproduce until they are about 18 months.

Female

Young

The hazards of hatching

Among reptiles, turtles lay the most eggs but care for them the least. Abandoned to the sand in which its egg was buried, this little hatchling (above) will fight alone to survive the world.

The young snake checks its surroundings with its tongue

The snake is in no hurry to leave the safety of its shell

2 Breaking the shell

During the seven to 15 weeks it takes to develop inside the egg, the young rat snake gets nourishment from the yolk. A day or two before hatching, the yolk sac is drawn into the body, and the yolk is absorbed into the snake's intestine. A small scar, like a belly button, shows the point where the embryo was joined to its food supply. As the young snake develops, a sharp but temporary "egg tooth" grows from the tip of its upper jaw. The baby snake uses this to pierce the egg shell and get its first view of the world.

3 Leaving the egg

Having tested its surroundings by flicking its tongue in and out (p.17), the young snake cautiously leaves its shell. It will be in no hurry to leave, however, and may stay with only its head poking out for a day or two. That way, if disturbed, it can always go back inside the egg.

5 Minor miracle

Fully out of its shell now, it seems amazing that such a long snake could ever have been packed inside such a small egg. The hatchlings, at 11–16 in (28–40 cm) long, may be up to seven times longer than their egg.

Scale tale

Skin forms a barrier between the outside world and our internal tissues. Reptiles' skin is dry and scaly; the scales on the outer layer are made of a horny substance called keratin—like fingernails. The outer skin is shed and renewed by cells in the inner layer. This allows snakes to grow, and replaces worn-out skin. Lizards and snakes have a "sloughing" time when they shed their skin. Most lizards shed skin in large flakes over a few days, while snakes slough the entire skin in one go.

Old skin is fragile and can break easily

Skin deep

Reptile skin varies from one species to another. In some lizards it may be bumpy, raised in spines, or form crests. In most snakes, the belly scales form wide, overlapping plates, which help it move (pp.52–53).

Counting scales
The pattern and number of scales on different parts of the head and body are valuable in helping specialists identify reptiles.

Caiman back

Smooth caiman belly skin

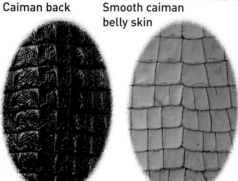

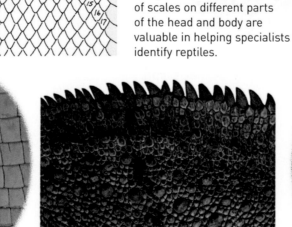

Horny-skinned armor
A caiman's back and tail has rough bony scales (scutes), strengthened by bony plates.

On the crest
Chameleon scales rise to a crest on its back.

Diggers
Smooth skink scales stop mud clinging.

Plated lizard
This lizard has bony plates under its scales.

New skin is smooth and shiny

New for old
Like reptiles, insects and other arthropods "molt" their tough outer skins, or exoskeletons, so they can grow. This cicada (right) has almost finished its final molt, producing an adult cicada with working wings. Its new exoskeleton is soft but soon hardens. Insects usually molt a set number of times, but some arthropods molt all their lives.

Old exoskeleton splits open along back

Wings expand as blood is pumped into them

Sloughing
The slow worm is a European legless lizard that sheds its skin in large pieces about four times a year. Adult lizards molt once a month when they are most active. Some lizards pull off their old skin with their mouth and swallow the strips, but the slow worm peels it off, like a snake. Most reptiles shed their skin throughout their lives, because they never stop growing.

Renewing the rattle
A rattlesnake's tail is made up of hollow segments of keratin. Every time the snake sheds its skin, a new segment is added to the rattle. When the tail shakes, the segments knock together to produce the rattle sound.

All in the eye
Several days before a snake sheds its skin, its eyes look cloudy, its skin is dull, it loses its appetite, and it may turn aggressive. Many snakes look for water to replace the body fluids they lose with their skins.

New skin for old
Snakes have no limbs, so they are able to slither out of their old skin within half an hour and leave it behind in one piece. The sloughing starts along the lips; the snake rubs its head on the ground to turn the skin back, and then slithers out, turning the skin inside out as it does so. The snake emerges, glistening in its new colors and scales.

Top

Adult rat snake skin

Young rat snake skin

Underside

Young snakes shed skin soon after they hatch, and about seven times in their first year

Snake selection

Snakes have no legs, eyelids, or eardrums, but can move quickly and sense their surroundings with special sensors. They live in water and on land, on all continents except Antarctica. More than 800 of the 2,500 species are poisonous, but only about 250 are dangerous to humans.

Bottoms up

When threatened, this harmless, burrowing snake from North America hides its head under its coiled body. It then waves its tail and shoots blood-stained liquid from its anal opening.

Back biter

This mildly venomous, rear-fanged, Madagascan hognose snake (right) rarely bites people but, if threatened, it flattens its neck (like a cobra) and hisses loudly. It shelters in burrows in grassland areas, eats small mammals and amphibians, and grows up to 5 ft (152 cm) long.

Night prowler

The Californian mountain kingsnake (below) is another snake that is harmless to people. In warm weather, it rests during the day and hunts at night for lizards, other snakes, and young birds. It can reach 40 in (102 cm) in length.

Corny

This nonpoisonous, American snake (above) is called the corn snake due to checkered markings on its belly that look like grain patterns on Indian corn. The longest corn snake measured was 72 in (183 cm).

Shrinking violet

This shy, gray-banded kingsnake (below) is rarely seen in the wild, but is a popular pet. It is 47 in (121 cm) when fully grown, and lives on a diet of lizards.

Stony look

In Greek mythology, Medusa's head was covered with snakes, and anyone who looked at her turned to stone.

Begone!
Legend says that St. Patrick banished snakes from Ireland to rid it of evil.

In the beginning
In some cultures, snakes are unpopular creatures. The Bible tells of Satan, as a serpent, tempting Eve with forbidden fruit in the Garden of Eden (below).

Stock still
The vine snake of Southeast Asia (above) spends hours hanging in trees, motionless and camouflaged. Its forward-facing eyes give it binocular vision, which helps it judge distances—especially when lunging at lizards.

Double bluff
This harmless Sinaloan milk snake (right) looks a lot like the highly venomous coral snake, deterring predators from eating it. Milk snakes are so-called due to a mistaken belief that they steal milk from cows.

The pits
The North American copperhead (left) is a member of the pit viper family. Like its rattlesnake relatives, the copperhead has a nasty bite. Its venom enters the victim's bloodstream, causing internal bleeding. However, people rarely die from the bites.

Eyes face forward

High flier
The flying snake is a rapid-moving tree snake from southern Asia. It hangs high up in the trees of thick forests, hunting lizards and frogs. It jumps between branches, and glides through the air. When it reaches the lower branches, it flattens its body to increase air resistance and slow down.

Loads of lizards

There are more than 5,500 species of lizard, including geckos, iguanas, chameleons, skinks, and monitors. It is the most successful reptile group, having evolved to many lifestyles: on the ground, in trees, in water, and as burrowers.

Mild moloch
The fierce-looking moloch (above) is a harmless, ant-eating lizard. Its spikes deter predators and collect dew, which condenses and runs into the lizard's mouth; it can then live for weeks without drinking.

Crest tale
The common iguana's crest runs like the teeth of a comb down the center of its back. These lizards are often seen basking in trees.

Blue mover
The blue-tongued skink (left) constantly flicks its blue tongue in and out. It gives birth to live young, and can move fast when necessary.

Komodo king
The Komodo dragon (above), a monitor lizard, is the world's largest living lizard; one dragon was 10 ft 2 in (3.1 m) long. It is found on just a few Indonesian islands.

Armor-plated
Plated lizards (above) have tough, bony plates under their scales (p.24). They normally have long tails, but this lizard's is regrowing after a narrow escape.

Flat as a pancake
This African lizard (below) has a flat body for slipping into crevices, and thick, protective scales. It jams itself into a rock crack and inflates its body so that predators can't pry it out.

Blinking geckos
Unlike most geckos, which have a fixed, transparent scale over each eye, leopard geckos (left) can blink. They also have sticky toe pads that can cling to smooth surfaces.

Color-conscious
Chameleons lead calm lives, which is fortunate as their main defense against enemies is the ability to change color. The male Jackson's chameleon (above) also has a three-pronged horn to help frighten away some foes.

Tree creeper
The glossy skinned, emerald tree skink (below right) lives in trees in Indonesia, rarely venturing to the ground.

Emerald tree skink

A toe-to-tail tale
Chameleons have remarkable toes, specialized for life in trees. The toes are arranged in a way that helps them clasp branches securely, while the tail twists and twines itself around twigs for extra support. The Madagascan chameleon (left), like others, also boasts a sticky-tipped tongue, which it can shoot out beyond the length of its body to catch insects and other small invertebrates.

Good influence
In Chinese art, the common lizard has evolved into a magnificent dragon. In Chinese folklore, it is the symbol of rebirth and fertility, and stars in Chinese street festivals.

Strong tail aids posture and balance

Eyed lizard
One of Europe's largest lizards at up to 2 ft 7 in (80 cm) long, the ey ocellated, lizard (above), from Europe a Africa, is a ground dweller, but can cl

Turtles and tortoises

Turtle god
In Hindu mythology, the god Vishnu, as the turtle Kurma, helped save Earth after a flood.

Reptiles with shells (chelonians) are found in most hot parts of the world. There are between 250 and 300 species. The shell protects and camouflages them. They live in saltwater, freshwater, and on land. Water-dwelling chelonians are called turtles (pond and river dwellers are sometimes called terrapins), and the rest are tortoises.

Galápagos giants
In 1835, Charles Darwin wrote about how giant tortoises had adapted to life on their own Galápagos island. There are two main groups: saddlebacks reach up to eat vegetation; domeshells graze on the ground.

Lonesome George
On Santa Cruz Island, in the Galápagos Islands, a giant tortoise nearly 3 ft (1 m) long appeared to be the only remaining giant tortoise from nearby Pinta Island. Attempts to find a female failed; George lived and died alone in 2012, aged around 90 years.

Dealing with pressure
Pond terrapins are mainly vegetarian and spend most of their time in water, although they do come onto land to bask in the sun. In some pond terrapins from southern Asia, the lungs are encased in bony boxes on the inside of the shell. This protects the lungs from the increased pressure underwater when the animals dive to great depths. The European pond terrapin is found in Europe, western Asia, and northwest Africa.

The carapace covers the back

The plastron covers the belly

Shell is made up of 59 to 61 bones, and is in two parts, the plastron and the carapace

Red ears
Red-eared terrapins, such as the one on the left, have a broad, red stripe on the side of the head. They are gentle, attractive creatures, and so make good pets. But, as pets, they seldom reach maturity because they do not get the vitamins and minerals they need. They live in ponds and rivers in the US, climbing on to logs to bask, where they may pile up on top of each other.

The red or yellow ear marking makes this turtle instantly recognizable

The plastron and carapace are joined on each side by a girdle bone

Lethal softy
The shell of soft-shelled turtles like this one (left) has no horny plates and feels like leather. In Africa, Asia, and North America, the turtles are usually found buried in mud in rivers and ponds. By stretching their long necks to the water's surface, they can breathe through a snorkel-like nose. They hide from enemies, but are fierce hunters, striking at lightning speed.

Record reptile
Leatherbacks are the largest living turtles. They breed in the Caribbean, then follow jellyfish, their main food, across the Atlantic. In 1988, this 2,016 lb (914 kg) leatherback (above) got caught in fishing lines and drowned. It washed up near Harlech, Wales; it is the biggest turtle ever recorded.

Hawksbill turtle shell

Large scales, called scutes, cover the bone of the shell

Starred tortoise shell

Radiated tortoise shell

Shells
Different lifestyles lead to different shells. Land tortoise shells are high-domed (like the radiated tortoise) or knobby (like the starred tortoise) to protect from predators' jaws. Turtles have streamlined shells for moving through water. Soft-shelled turtles have the flattest shells, for hiding in mud.

Turtle tank

In folklore, the alligator snapping turtle was thought to be a cross between a common turtle and an alligator. It is a ferocious turtle, with a powerful head and knifelike jaws. It spends nearly all its time in water. When fishing for prey, the turtle lies motionless on the riverbed, with its mouth open. It will eat anything it can catch: snails, clams, and other turtles. It is one of the world's largest freshwater turtles, growing up to 26 in (66 cm) long and weighing up to 200 lb (91 kg).

Wormlike appendage

Sharp jaws used to cut prey

Wiggly worm
One of the most remarkable features of the alligator snapper is the wormlike appendage on the end of its tongue. This fills with blood that colors it red so it looks like an earthworm, like the one shown right. When hungry, the turtle lies very still on the river bed, opens its mouth, and wiggles the "worm." Unwary passing prey are tempted by the bait, and the jaws of the turtle snap shut.

Turtle rises on its forelegs when faced by an aggressor

Sucked to death

The matamata turtle (right) from South America, like the
alligator snapper, lies on river beds waiting for prey. When
prey approaches, the matamata expands its throat, creating
a current that sucks the prey into its jaws.

*Ridged and
roughened shell
provides both
protection and
camouflage*

*Very powerful forelegs are
often used to hold prey*

Unsafe to bathe

The alligator snapper, found in the southeastern US, looks
like a stone, especially when its ridged shell is covered by
algae. It relies on this camouflage to trap its prey. Careless
bathers in this river (above) could suffer damaged toes from
its bladelike jaws. It is unlikely, however, because the turtles
are rare, endangered due to illegal collection and pollution.

Crocodile clan

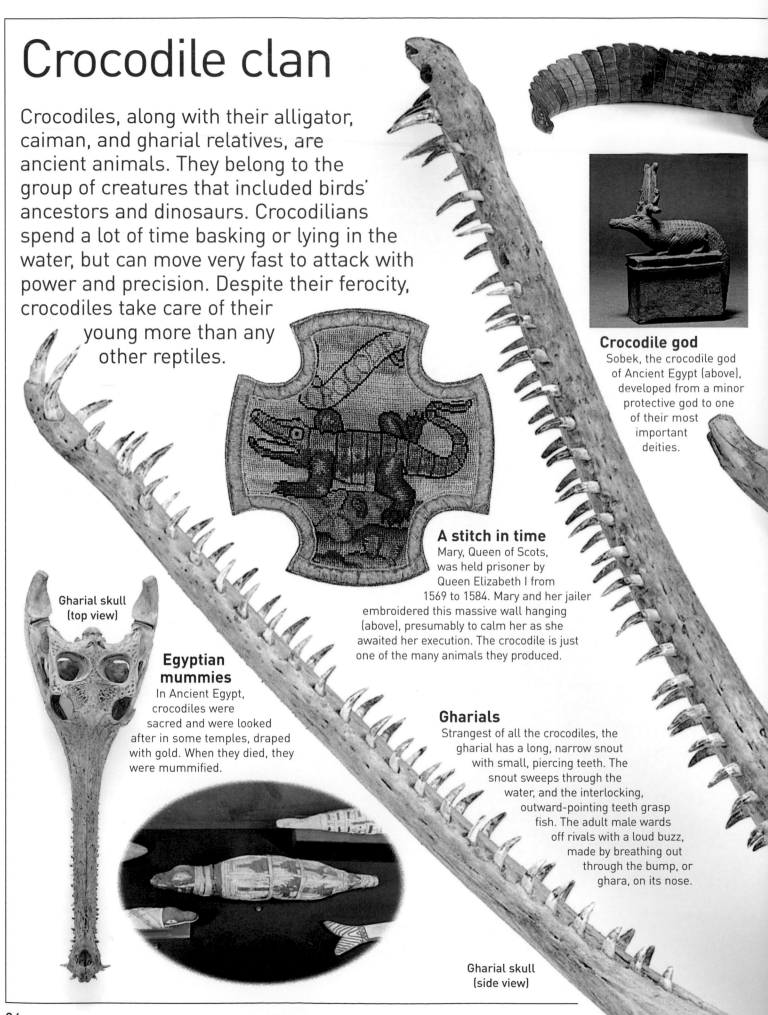

Crocodiles, along with their alligator, caiman, and gharial relatives, are ancient animals. They belong to the group of creatures that included birds' ancestors and dinosaurs. Crocodilians spend a lot of time basking or lying in the water, but can move very fast to attack with power and precision. Despite their ferocity, crocodiles take care of their young more than any other reptiles.

Crocodile god
Sobek, the crocodile god of Ancient Egypt (above), developed from a minor protective god to one of their most important deities.

A stitch in time
Mary, Queen of Scots, was held prisoner by Queen Elizabeth I from 1569 to 1584. Mary and her jailer embroidered this massive wall hanging (above), presumably to calm her as she awaited her execution. The crocodile is just one of the many animals they produced.

Gharial skull (top view)

Egyptian mummies
In Ancient Egypt, crocodiles were sacred and were looked after in some temples, draped with gold. When they died, they were mummified.

Gharials
Strangest of all the crocodiles, the gharial has a long, narrow snout with small, piercing teeth. The snout sweeps through the water, and the interlocking, outward-pointing teeth grasp fish. The adult male wards off rivals with a loud buzz, made by breathing out through the bump, or ghara, on its nose.

Gharial skull (side view)

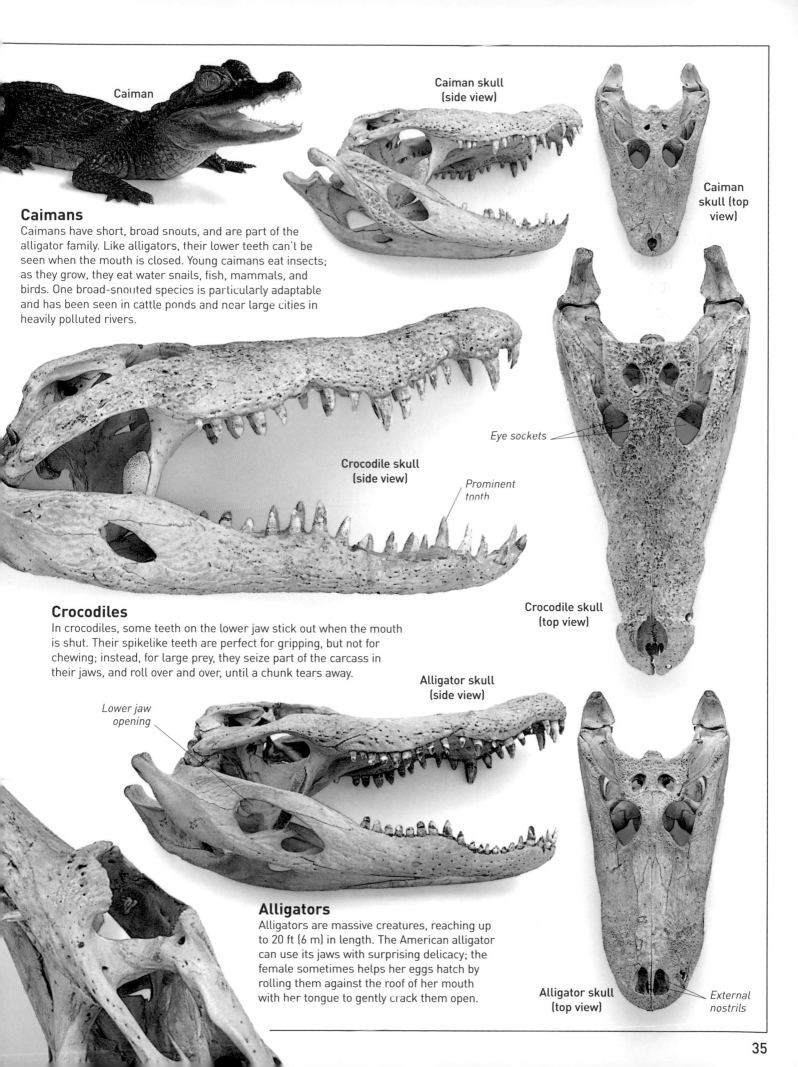

Caiman

Caiman skull (side view)

Caiman skull (top view)

Caimans

Caimans have short, broad snouts, and are part of the alligator family. Like alligators, their lower teeth can't be seen when the mouth is closed. Young caimans eat insects; as they grow, they eat water snails, fish, mammals, and birds. One broad-snouted species is particularly adaptable and has been seen in cattle ponds and near large cities in heavily polluted rivers.

Eye sockets

Crocodile skull (side view)

Prominent tooth

Crocodile skull (top view)

Crocodiles

In crocodiles, some teeth on the lower jaw stick out when the mouth is shut. Their spikelike teeth are perfect for gripping, but not for chewing; instead, for large prey, they seize part of the carcass in their jaws, and roll over and over, until a chunk tears away.

Alligator skull (side view)

Lower jaw opening

Alligators

Alligators are massive creatures, reaching up to 20 ft (6 m) in length. The American alligator can use its jaws with surprising delicacy; the female sometimes helps her eggs hatch by rolling them against the roof of her mouth with her tongue to gently crack them open.

Alligator skull (top view)

External nostrils

35

Tuatara

The tuatara is described as a "living fossil" because it is the sole survivor of an extinct group of animals; its closest relatives died out millions of years ago, and no one knows why the tuatara alone survived. It lives on small islands off the coast of New Zealand; otherwise, it is only found fossilized in rocks. It is active at night and inhabits burrows, often shared with seabirds. It looks like a lizard, but is different: it can function well in a cool climate, and its lower internal temperature means its body is slow to convert food into energy, resulting in a very slow growth rate.

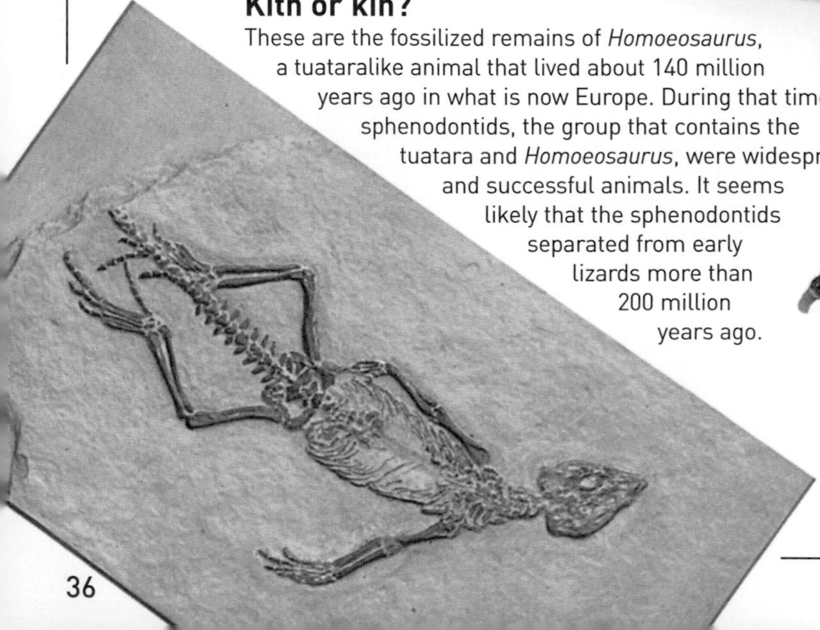

Male

Female

Kith or kin?

These are the fossilized remains of *Homoeosaurus*, a tuataralike animal that lived about 140 million years ago in what is now Europe. During that time, sphenodontids, the group that contains the tuatara and *Homoeosaurus*, were widespread and successful animals. It seems likely that the sphenodontids separated from early lizards more than 200 million years ago.

Short, strong legs, suitable for excavating burrows

Tuatara, a Māori word meaning "peaks on the back," refers to the crest that runs down the back and tail

Resurrection

Another living fossil is the coelacanth (which means "hollow spine")—a group of fish that lived from 300 to 90 million years ago. They were thought to be extinct, and were known only as fossils—until 1938, when a live coelacanth was caught off the coast of South Africa. The coelacanth "home" was discovered 14 years later, in deep waters near the Comoro Islands, northwest of Madagascar.

Growing old together

Male tuatara grow to a length of about 2 ft (61 cm); females are slightly shorter. Tuatara reach sexual maturity at about 20 years of age, and can live 120 years. They have no external ear openings, and the male has no sexual organ. After mating, the female stores the sperm in her body for a year, and then lays between five and 15 eggs in a shallow burrow. The eggs hatch after 15 months.

A third "eye" is sensitive to light. Visible in the young animal, the skin thickens over this organ in the adult. It may regulate the "biological clock" of the tuatara and also possibly acts as a thermostat

Teeth are part of the jawbone, which has serrated edges

Bony arches

Skull structure

The tuatara's skull has two bony arches that frame the back, rather like a crocodilian's. In most lizards, the lower arch is missing; in snakes and many burrowing lizards, both arches have gone.

Echidna (spiny anteater)

Duck-billed platypus

Odd ones out

The duck-billed platypus and the echidna are not strictly "living fossils," but they are primitive and unusual mammals. The platypus has a duck bill and beaver tail; the spiky echidna resembles a hedgehog. Like reptiles, both mammals lay eggs.

A bite to eat

Most reptiles are meat-eaters. Crocodiles and snakes are all carnivores, but some snakes have specialized diets and eat only birds' eggs (pp.44–45) or fish eggs (eaten by sea snakes). Many lizards feed on insects, mammals, birds, and other reptiles, but large iguanas, some big skinks, and a few agamids are mostly vegetarian. Tortoises eat a variety of plants, and occasionally eat meat. Freshwater turtles often eat worms, snails, and fish. Sea turtles feed on jellyfish, crabs, mollusks, and fish, but also eat plants.

Slow but sure

Few tortoises or turtles have the speed or agility to catch fast-moving prey; most feed on plants, or slow-moving animals like mollusks, worms, and insect larvae. They make the most of food that is nearby. The spur-thighed tortoise also nibbles on any dead animal it finds.

Hook meets his end

In J. M. Barrie's *Peter Pan*, Captain Hook is haunted by the crocodile who ate his hand and wants more. Usually warned of its presence by a ticking clock in its stomach, Hook is finally tricked.

Crocodile larder

Nile crocodiles may share a large animal carcass. Crocodile stomachs are basketball-sized, so crocs cannot eat a big animal all at once. Instead, prey is often left in one spot for finishing later. This led to the belief that crocodiles like to eat rotten meat; in fact, they prefer fresh meat.

Armlets

Stones

Bangle

Pieces of turtle shell

Porcupine quills

Stomach store

Crocodiles often devour hard, heavy objects, such as stones and pieces of metal (above). The objects may be eaten to help the crocodile grind and digest its food.

Shed tooth

Tooth in use

Developing tooth

Developing teeth

Mammals have two sets of teeth—baby "milk" teeth, and an adult set. Crocodiles shed teeth throughout their lives, and new ones constantly replace old ones.

Eyed lizards are mainly ground dwellers, but they are also excellent climbers.

Crickets and grasshoppers are eyed lizards' favorite food.

Crispy cricket

After a rapid chase, the eyed lizard grabs a cricket with its jaws (above), and violently shakes it to stun it. The lizard passes the cricket to the back of its mouth. Its jaw moves over the prey in a series of snapping movements; its teeth grip and release the cricket as the jaw moves. The lizard must eat fast—the cricket may not be totally stunned and will try to escape. The majority of lizards are insect eaters, and, in some areas, are important in keeping insect populations down.

Sharpshooters

With tongues longer than their bodies, chameleons are the sharpshooters of the lizard world. The tongue is hollow and unforked, with a large, sticky tip. A contracting muscle shoots it from the mouth at lightning speed with great accuracy to catch prey. Different muscles draw the tongue back into the mouth, where it is kept bunched up until it is needed again.

A tight squeeze

All snakes eat meat and have developed different ways of killing their food. Some kill their prey with venom; pythons and boas, which mainly eat mammals, kill by constriction—by coiling their bodies around their prey and squeezing just enough to match the prey's breathing movements. This makes it hard for the prey to breathe and it finally suffocates. Any mammal from a mouse to a deer is chosen, depending on the size of the snake.

Tintin to the rescue!
There are Asian and African records of large python species killing and eating humans. In a *Tintin* book, Zorrino the guide is in danger of being eaten (left), but is saved just in time by Tintin.

Dangerous act
Music hall and circus performers who dance with constrictors are taking a great risk. This drawing (above) is of a dancer who was nearly suffocated by a python—and was rescued only seconds before certain death.

2 Deadly embrace
The constricting snake reacts to every tiny movement and heartbeat of the rat, tightening its grip until the rat's heart ceases beating. Only then will the snake release its hold. Death is fairly quick, and bones are rarely broken. The snake positions the rat for swallowing headfirst.

3 Big mouth
The snake's powerful, flexible jaws move easily: upper and lower jaws move from side to side; backward-pointing teeth grip tightly. As the jaws move over the head of the rat, it looks like the snake is walking over its food.

4 Safety first
A small animal may disappear in just one or two gulps, but it can take an hour or more for larger prey. The snake's swallowing is mainly automatic—prey is drawn in by trunk muscles. But it can regurgitate food to escape any danger.

Body can expand to allow for large prey

5 Tight fit
Now, most of the rat has disappeared. The flexible ligament—an elastic muscle that connects the two halves of the snake's lower jaw—allows the snake to open its mouth wide. As the lower jaws are forced apart, the muscle between them stretches to the shape of the prey.

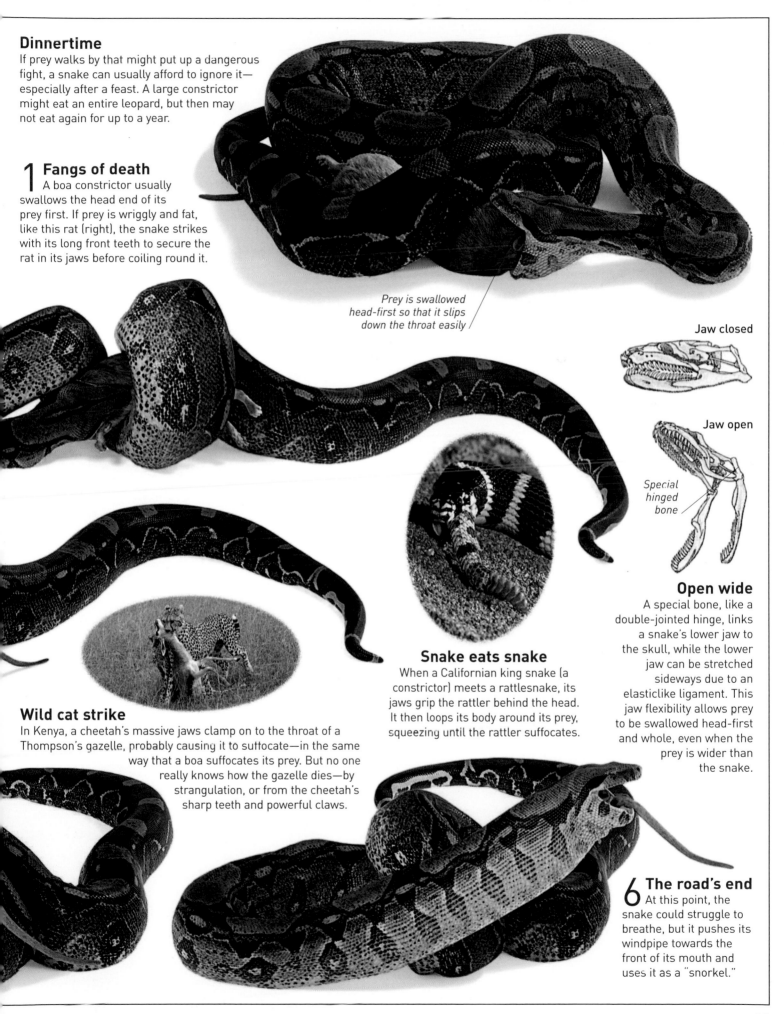

Dinnertime

If prey walks by that might put up a dangerous fight, a snake can usually afford to ignore it—especially after a feast. A large constrictor might eat an entire leopard, but then may not eat again for up to a year.

1 Fangs of death

A boa constrictor usually swallows the head end of its prey first. If prey is wriggly and fat, like this rat (right), the snake strikes with its long front teeth to secure the rat in its jaws before coiling round it.

Prey is swallowed head-first so that it slips down the throat easily

Jaw closed

Jaw open

Special hinged bone

Open wide

A special bone, like a double-jointed hinge, links a snake's lower jaw to the skull, while the lower jaw can be stretched sideways due to an elasticlike ligament. This jaw flexibility allows prey to be swallowed head-first and whole, even when the prey is wider than the snake.

Snake eats snake

When a Californian king snake (a constrictor) meets a rattlesnake, its jaws grip the rattler behind the head. It then loops its body around its prey, squeezing until the rattler suffocates.

Wild cat strike

In Kenya, a cheetah's massive jaws clamp on to the throat of a Thompson's gazelle, probably causing it to suffocate—in the same way that a boa suffocates its prey. But no one really knows how the gazelle dies—by strangulation, or from the cheetah's sharp teeth and powerful claws.

6 The road's end

At this point, the snake could struggle to breathe, but it pushes its windpipe towards the front of its mouth and uses it as a "snorkel."

Poisoned bite

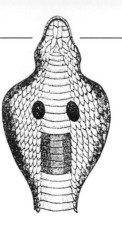

Apart from two lizards, snakes are the only poisonous, or venomous, reptiles. Poisonous snakes are found around the world, but the most venomous live in tropical areas. They inject poison, or venom, into prey using special teeth or fangs. In the most lethal, such as sea snakes, vipers, and cobras, the fangs are at the front of the upper jaw; in other snakes, they can be at the back. The venom affects the prey's nervous system, tissues, blood, or all three. It subdues its victims so the snake can kill it to eat, or flee if it's a predator.

Cheek muscles contract, forcing venom out

Extracting venom from a snake

"Milking" snakes for venom is still done in parts of the world, because venom is used to produce serum (fluid used to stop the effects of poison) against snake bites. The snake, held by the head, is made to bite through tissue over a container. Gentle pressure on the venom sac in its cheeks then forces it to eject venom.

Rattlesnakes

The extremely venomous rattlesnake is sometimes known as a pit viper due to the heat-sensitive pit between its nostrils and eyes; this enables it to locate the warm bodies of prey in the cool, dark night. A rattlesnake may shed its skin and add a new rattle two or three times a year—which disproves the myth that you can tell a snake's age by the number of rattles on its tail.

Other poisoners

Sea snakes include some of the world's most venomous species, although they have small fangs, and rarely attack humans. On land, there are two species of poisonous lizard—the Gila monster and the Mexican beaded lizard. Both are found in southwestern US and Mexico. Their venom comes from saliva glands in the lower jaw, which they chew into the victim.

Sea snake

Gila monster

Fang facts

Rattlesnake fangs are folded back against the roof of the mouth until needed, when they rotate forward. Replacement fang pairs are arranged behind them, in the roof of the mouth.

Venom passes through tube

Hole in the tip of the fang

Venom sac

Killer shrew

The short-tailed shrew is one of the few mammals with a poisonous bite. When it bites into prey—usually insects and earthworms—the venom in its saliva will kill in seconds.

Star performers
Snakes have featured in literature for centuries. In Shakespeare's *Antony and Cleopatra* (left), Cleopatra commits suicide using an asp (poisonous Egyptian serpent). Snakes also appear in films, such as *True Grit* (below), where John Wayne examines a snake bite on Kim Darby's hand.

Antony and Cleopatra.

Snake stones
Once wrongly thought to absorb venom and so cure snake bites, snake stones were made of burned bone, chalk, horn, or other absorbent materials.

Special scales make up rattle

Hollow segments lock together

Rattle

Rapid vibration produces a sizzling sound

Egg eaters

Some snakes only eat eggs, and have become specialized for the task. Small eggs, especially soft-shelled ones laid by lizards and some other snakes, are easy for a snake to split open with their teeth and eat. Larger, hard-shelled eggs, such as birds' eggs, need special treatment. True egg-eating snakes eat only birds' eggs, swallowed whole because they have few teeth. Toothlike spines along their backbone crack open the egg as it moves down the throat.

Diet of eggs

In some parts of the world, birds only lay eggs at certain times of the year, and so a snake may have to go a long time without food. Fortunately, egg-eating snakes can regurgitate (bring up) eggshell so that no space is wasted in its stomach. This means it can eat as many eggs as it finds, and doesn't waste energy digesting the shell.

2 Swallow hard

The egg is passing down the snake's throat. The skin on the side of the neck is very elastic, and at this stage the egg is still unbroken.

Head arches down, pushing the egg against the bony inner spines to puncture the shell

Finely interlinked scales separate as the skin stretches

3 Spiny bones

The passage of the egg has now been stopped by the toothlike spines on the underside of the neck bones.

The "bulge" is noticeably smaller

A valve at the entrance to the stomach accepts yolks and liquids, but rejects pieces of shell

4 Going down

Once the egg is punctured, the snake's body muscles work in waves to squeeze out the contents, which continue on to the stomach. The snake then bends its body into S-shaped curves to force the eggshell back toward its mouth.

5 And up it comes

It can take five minutes to an hour, depending on the size of the egg, for it to be completely swallowed. Finally, the snake gapes widely and the compacted shell fragments are brought up, still held together by the sticky egg membranes.

The jagged edges of the shell pieces are stuck together. All the goodness in the egg has been drained

Regurgitated shell

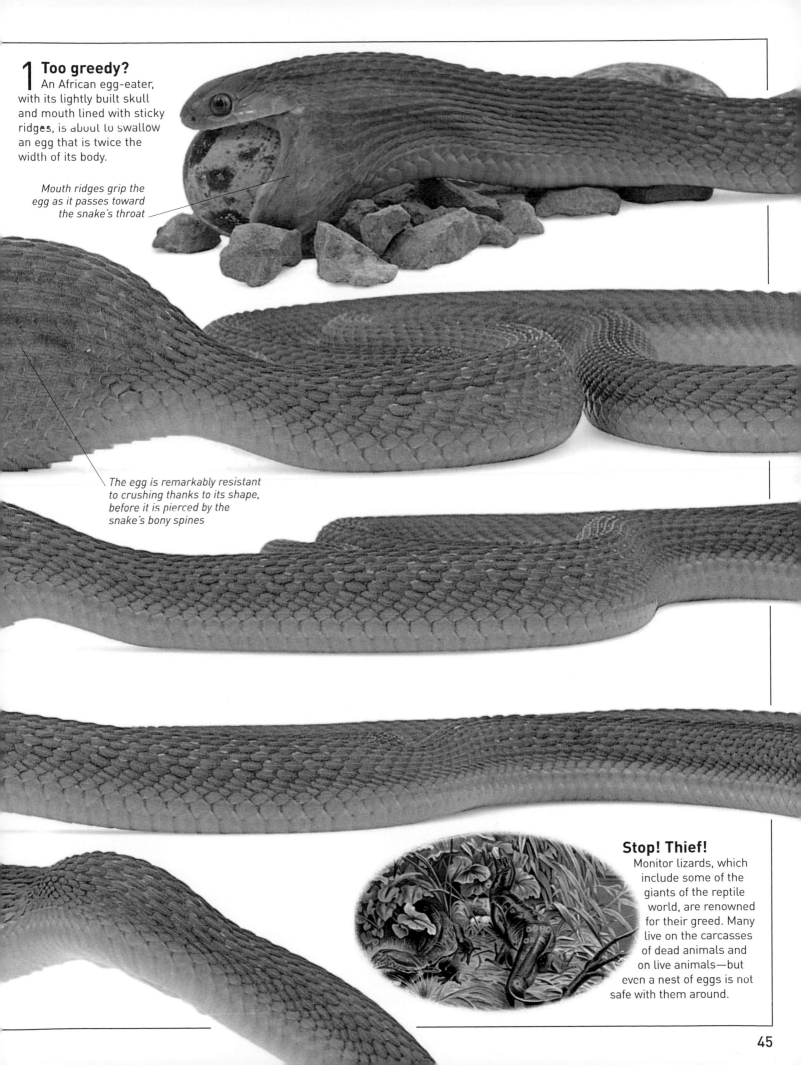

1 Too greedy?

An African egg-eater, with its lightly built skull and mouth lined with sticky ridges, is about to swallow an egg that is twice the width of its body.

Mouth ridges grip the egg as it passes toward the snake's throat

The egg is remarkably resistant to crushing thanks to its shape, before it is pierced by the snake's bony spines

Stop! Thief!

Monitor lizards, which include some of the giants of the reptile world, are renowned for their greed. Many live on the carcasses of dead animals and on live animals—but even a nest of eggs is not safe with them around.

Survival

Reptiles use many methods to frighten away enemies. Some inflate themselves with air, then blow it out with a hiss. Several lizards and some snakes sacrifice their tail to save their head and trunk. Some American horned lizards swell up and squirt blood (which may irritate other animals' eyes) from tiny eye capillaries. Some use camouflage to avoid being seen in the first place. The armadillo lizard from South Africa coils up into a tight ball to protect its soft belly; thick, spiny scales along its head, back, and tail are a perfect shield.

On guard

The Australian frilled lizard (below) has a "frill" of loose skin, normally kept folded flat, attached to its neck. When startled by a predator, the lizard erects this rufflike collar, which can be four times the width of its body. If challenged, the lizard will also bob its head, lash its tail, and wave its legs. While most lizards under attack try to escape, the frilled lizard meets danger head on.

Gaping mouth expands the neck frill. The wider the mouth is opened, the more erect the frill becomes

Frill fully erected to scare aggressors

Tail is lashed back and forth

Extended claws and flexed feet provide strong balance

Stinky stinkpot

The skunk is a mammal that is well known for the foul smell it makes when threatened. The stinkpot is a North American turtle that is both smelly and aggressive—so it is unlikely to be set upon by many predators. When frightened, its stink is produced by a pair of glands in the soft skin of the thighs.

Stinkpot

Skunk

Survival kit

To survive adverse conditions, people use special clothes and equipment. Reptiles cannot survive extreme temperatures, but they can adapt to changing weather within their environment.

The tale of a tail

When grabbed by the tail, most lizards will shed it to avoid death. Several lizards wiggle their tail when first attacked, which helps confuse the predator. The vertebrae, or small backbones, along the tail have special cracks where the tail can break off. When the tail is grasped, the muscles, which are also arranged for separating, contract and cause a vertebra to break off.

Fracture points along the tail

1 Breaking free

This tree skink gave up its tail to a predator. The shed tail part often twitches for several minutes after shedding, confusing the attacker so the lizard can escape.

Tail has been recently shed

New tail looks the same on the outside, but has a simple tube of cartilage instead of vertebrae on the inside

2 Growing stronger

In two months, a new tail-part is noticeable. However, the new tail doesn't replace the stored food that was in the original tail, built up for a time when food may be scarce, such as in winter or a dry season. It's therefore not surprising that some species live longer when they have a complete tail.

3 New for old

After eight months, the tail has almost fully regrown. It can be broken off again, but only in the old part, where there are vertebrae. Growing a new tail uses a lot of energy that could have been put to better use.

Fully regrown tail

Playing dead

When all else fails, some snakes will pretend to be dead. When this European grass snake (right) meets an enemy, it puffs and hisses loudly. If this does not scare off the attacker, the snake rolls over onto its back, wriggles (as if dying), and then lies still, with its mouth wide open and tongue hanging out. Even if the snake is turned over, it will stay "dead," not moving, so as not to give the game away.

Blending in

Many reptiles blend in with their surroundings. This is known as camouflage, and it helps reptiles avoid being spotted by both prey and predators. In some reptiles, the skin colors match their surroundings; in others, skin pattern helps to hide the body's outline; in a few, the animal's shape improves camouflage—such as the side fringes and leaf-shaped tails of tree-living geckos.

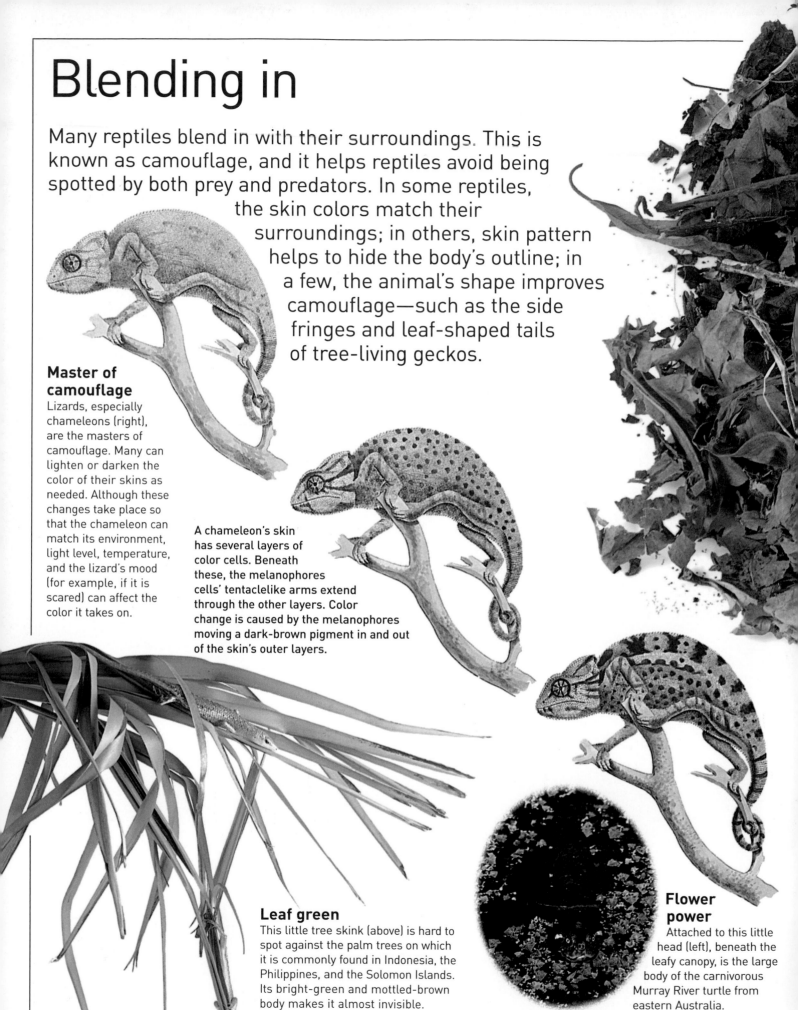

Master of camouflage

Lizards, especially chameleons (right), are the masters of camouflage. Many can lighten or darken the color of their skins as needed. Although these changes take place so that the chameleon can match its environment, light level, temperature, and the lizard's mood (for example, if it is scared) can affect the color it takes on.

A chameleon's skin has several layers of color cells. Beneath these, the melanophores cells' tentaclelike arms extend through the other layers. Color change is caused by the melanophores moving a dark-brown pigment in and out of the skin's outer layers.

Leaf green

This little tree skink (above) is hard to spot against the palm trees on which it is commonly found in Indonesia, the Philippines, and the Solomon Islands. Its bright-green and mottled-brown body makes it almost invisible.

Flower power

Attached to this little head (left), beneath the leafy canopy, is the large body of the carnivorous Murray River turtle from eastern Australia.

Double trouble

Lying still in the leaf litter of tropical Africa's forests, these gaboon vipers (above) are nearly invisible in the dappled light and shade, as they lie in wait for rodents, frogs, and birds. Yet, when seen out of its leafy environment, its vivid markings are strikingly obvious. Although unaggressive and unlikely to attack, its bite would be dangerously venomous to anyone unfortunate enough to tread on it. In fact, the fangs of the gaboon viper are the longest of any snake—up to 2 in (50 mm) in a 6-ft (1.8-m) viper.

Gaboon viper

Hidden depths

The black caiman is often mistaken for rocks as it lies in muddy water. Staying unseen helps it when it is looking for food.

Lots of legs

Legs and feet are vital in many reptiles' lives—although snakes and some lizards do well without them. Legs and feet are adapted to a reptile's habitat. Desert lizards often have long scales fringing their toes, which help them walk on soft sand. Webbed feet, or paddle-shaped limbs, help aquatic turtles swim. In other swimming reptiles, such as crocodiles, the tail propels them forward and the limbs are folded back, out of the way.

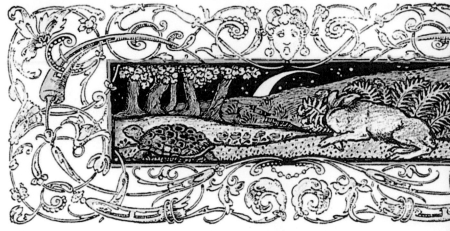

The hare and the tortoise

In the famous Aesop fable, the hare is so confident of winning his race with the slow and ponderous tortoise that he falls asleep by the wayside, and the tortoise crosses the finishing line first. It is certainly true that although tortoises are slow, they make steady progress and can travel long distances, seldom stopping for a rest.

Legs of all sorts

A reptile's feet reflect its lifestyle. The slightly webbed back feet of caimans helps propel them through the water. The powerful feet and legs of lizards such as plated lizards and monitors are good for digging. The sharp-clawed toes of the girdled lizards provide grip when climbing flaking rock surfaces. In some of the smaller skinks, the tiny limbs barely support the animal.

Caiman

Plated lizard

Monitor lizard

African girdled lizard

Blue-tongued skink

All five toes spread out to achieve maximum grip

Geckos have no trouble moving vertically or hanging horizontally

Get a grip

The tokay (right) is a fairly large gecko from east Asia that is so-called because it makes a noise that sounds like "tokay." It is one of the best lizard climbers and has no difficulty scaling a wall, running across a ceiling, and even clinging to a sheet of glass. It grips by using pads on the ends of its fingers and toes. The pads are covered by thousands of microscopic hairlike structures, which rub the surface on which the animal is walking, allowing it to cling to almost any surface.

Elongated body resembles that of a snake

Loss of legs

This glass lizard (above) is often mistaken for a snake. It has no front legs, and only tiny remnants of back legs. Many lizards, particularly burrowing types, have evolved in the same way: loss of legs and a lengthened body, which is better equipped for a life underground. Some legless lizards, like the glass lizard, live above ground in rocky habitats or thick vegetation.

Vestigial limbs (small remnants of hind legs) are of no use in movement, but the male may use them in courtship to stimulate the female

Little limbs

In most snakes, all traces of limbs have been lost. In some of the more primitive groups, such as boas and pythons, tiny remnants remain of hip bones and hind limbs. These appear as small "claws" at the the tail base, on either side of the vent, or anal opening.

Tokay gecko, climbing

Ground control

Most lizards rely on swiftness and agility to hunt and get out of trouble. They usually use all four limbs—their legs and feet are specially adapted to where they live. Turtles have no need for speed; their powerful legs carry the heavy, protective shell and propel them forward slowly but surely. Snakes move efficiently on land in a variety of ways, depending on their surroundings. Crocodilians are most at home in water; when on land, they crawl, dragging their bellies along the ground.

High-speed sprinter
The six-lined racerunner lizard, found in North America, is one of the fastest reptiles on land. It can reach a speed of 11 mph (18 kph).

Palm flexed against the ground

Back legs provide most of the thrust

Moving foot

Three feet are kept on the ground, while only one foot moves when the lizard is advancing at a slow pace

Tegu lizard

Long tail helps lizard balance when running on its hind legs

Alert crested water dragon, standing on all four feet

3 Two at a time
When a lizard breaks into a trot, the body is supported by two legs at a time (the diagonal pairs). There may even be times when both front feet and one hind foot are off the ground.

Two legs are better than four
This crested water dragon (right) from Asia lives mainly in trees near water. If disturbed when on the ground, it may rear up on its hind legs and run while upright. Several lizards use this type of bipedal (two-legged) locomotion; they are able to run much faster on two legs than four.

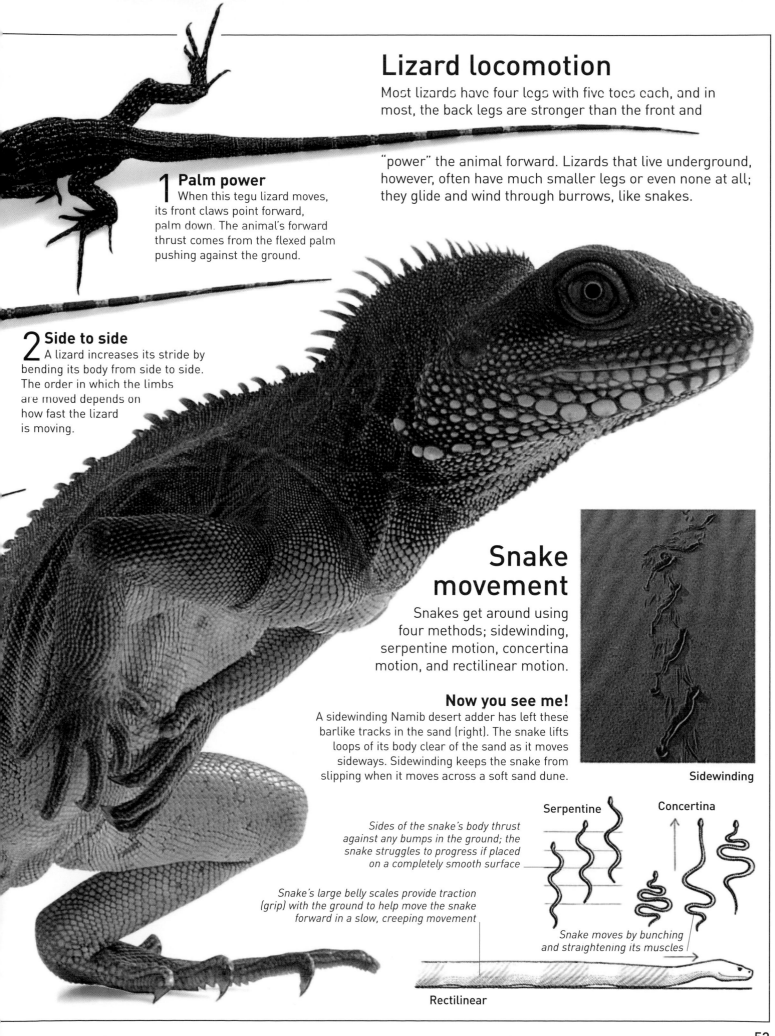

Lizard locomotion

Most lizards have four legs with five toes each, and in most, the back legs are stronger than the front and "power" the animal forward. Lizards that live underground, however, often have much smaller legs or even none at all; they glide and wind through burrows, like snakes.

1 Palm power
When this tegu lizard moves, its front claws point forward, palm down. The animal's forward thrust comes from the flexed palm pushing against the ground.

2 Side to side
A lizard increases its stride by bending its body from side to side. The order in which the limbs are moved depends on how fast the lizard is moving.

Snake movement

Snakes get around using four methods; sidewinding, serpentine motion, concertina motion, and rectilinear motion.

Now you see me!
A sidewinding Namib desert adder has left these barlike tracks in the sand (right). The snake lifts loops of its body clear of the sand as it moves sideways. Sidewinding keeps the snake from slipping when it moves across a soft sand dune.

Sidewinding

Serpentine

Concertina

Sides of the snake's body thrust against any bumps in the ground; the snake struggles to progress if placed on a completely smooth surface

Snake's large belly scales provide traction (grip) with the ground to help move the snake forward in a slow, creeping movement

Snake moves by bunching and straightening its muscles

Rectilinear

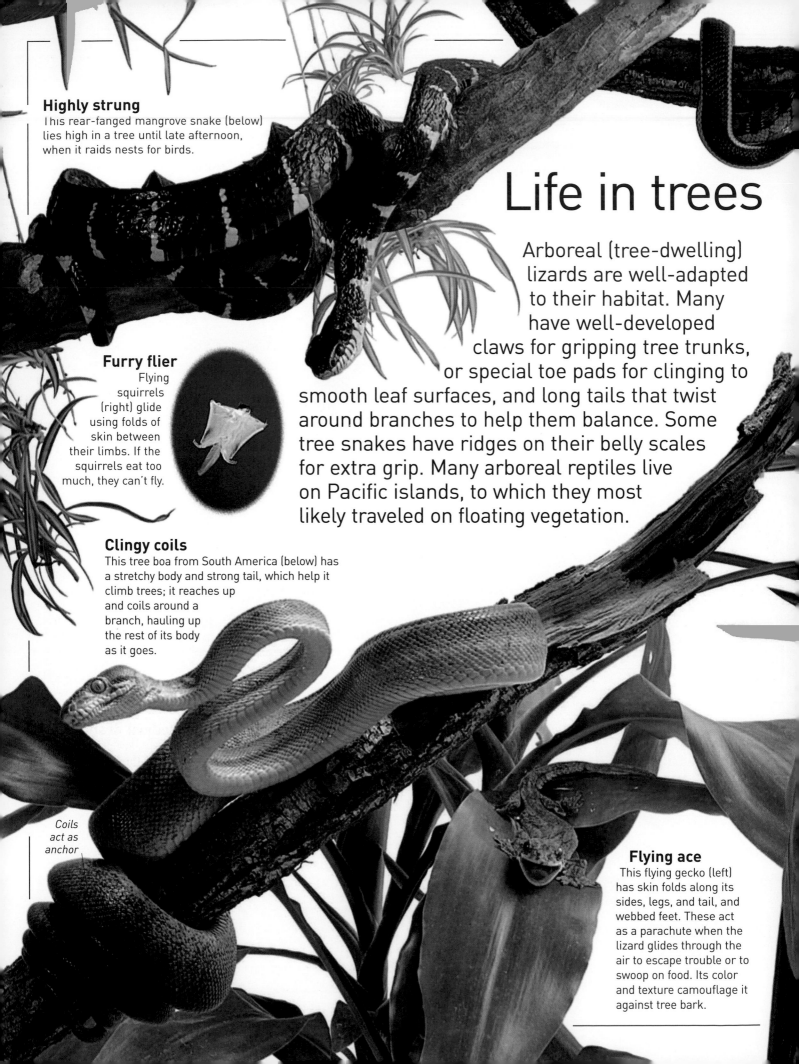

Highly strung

This rear-fanged mangrove snake (below) lies high in a tree until late afternoon, when it raids nests for birds.

Life in trees

Arboreal (tree-dwelling) lizards are well-adapted to their habitat. Many have well-developed claws for gripping tree trunks, or special toe pads for clinging to smooth leaf surfaces, and long tails that twist around branches to help them balance. Some tree snakes have ridges on their belly scales for extra grip. Many arboreal reptiles live on Pacific islands, to which they most likely traveled on floating vegetation.

Furry flier

Flying squirrels (right) glide using folds of skin between their limbs. If the squirrels eat too much, they can't fly.

Clingy coils

This tree boa from South America (below) has a stretchy body and strong tail, which help it climb trees; it reaches up and coils around a branch, hauling up the rest of its body as it goes.

Coils act as anchor

Flying ace

This flying gecko (left) has skin folds along its sides, legs, and tail, and webbed feet. These act as a parachute when the lizard glides through the air to escape trouble or to swoop on food. Its color and texture camouflage it against tree bark.

Hanging on
An emerald green tree boa catches a bird (left) while coiled around a branch to support itself.

Cooling down
The trinket snake from India (above) is a part-time tree-dweller. In hot weather, it shelters in termite mounds or under rocks on the ground. In cooler weather, it moves up into trees and bushes.

Garden lizard

Bloodsucker
The garden lizard (above) has a long, slender tail and a body like a chameleon's. It changes color rapidly – its head especially, which may turn red. The lips of some turn so red that the lizards are nicknamed bloodsuckers.

Daredevil dragons
Flying dragons (below) parachute through the air using flaps of skin stretched over elongated ribs. These "wings" fold back when not in use.

Day duty
All geckos are good climbers, because their toes' friction pads help them grip. Most are nocturnal, and eat insects and fruit, but some, such as this one (right), are active by day and eat palm flowers' nectar.

Waterproofed

Reptiles are mainly land animals, but some live in water. Crocodilians, a few marine lizards, some snakes, and terrapins and turtles all spend much of their lives submerged. Most reptiles lay their eggs on dry land—or the eggs would drown—but some sea snakes around Asia, northern Australia, and the Pacific islands give birth to live young that can swim and come up for air. Different reptiles use their watery home differently: crocodilians use it to swim, hunt, and cool off; marine iguanas feed on its algae.

Tail walking
If a crocodile is being chased, or if it is giving chase, it can move very fast, even leaping out of the water. This "tail walk" demonstrates how graceful and at ease the animal is in water.

Snorkel snout
In calm water, an alligator (above) can rest, submerged, with just its nose disk above the surface to breathe. When it dives, special muscles and flaps close over the nostrils and ears. Well-developed eyelids protect the eyes, and a flap of transparent skin shoots across the eyes so it can see underwater. Another flap in the throat keeps water from entering the lungs.

Caiman lies still in the water as a defense against predators and in order to catch prey

Caiman

Eyes are high on the head

Jesu Cristo lizard

When frightened, this little basilisk lizard (below) drops onto the water. The broad soles and fringe of scales on its feet enable it to scuttle across the surface on its back legs. As the lizard loses speed, it sinks through the water's surface and swims to safety.

Monsters of the deep

Myths of strange creatures living in deep waters, such as in Scotland's Loch Ness, have been around for centuries. The appearance of some water reptiles probably accounts for the myths.

Basilisk lizard

The speed of the basilisk allows it to run on the surface of the water

The wet look

People aren't adapted for survival in water. Unlike reptiles, our skin and bodies need protection from cold-water temperatures.

Soft backs

Water turtles tend to have lower, more streamlined shells than land turtles, and are therefore better suited to swimming. Soft-shelled turtles (above) have the flattest shells—perfect for hiding beneath sand and mud on the riverbed. Their feet have long, webbed toes that give them extra thrust to move through the water.

Nostrils lie just above water level

Water baby

This young caiman (left) is very well-adapted to life in water. Its eyes, nostrils, and ears are high on its head so that it can breathe and see, while the rest of its body lies hidden underwater. This is an advantage when hunting prey that comes to the water's edge to drink. The caiman, like all other crocodilians, is a good swimmer. Tucking its legs and webbed feet against its sides, it can propel itself forward with its powerful tail. The caiman depends on water; if it lies in the hot sun without cooling off in water, it will die.

Underwater breathing

All turtles have lungs, but aquatic types can also breathe through their skin and throat lining. Some can tolerate very low oxygen levels and survive for weeks underwater, but this little red-eared terrapin (right) can only last for two or three hours.

Red-eared terrapin

Best of enemies

Reptiles have a number of enemies. Large birds, such as owls and eagles, and some mammals, such as hedgehogs and cats, all prey on snakes and lizards. Some reptiles, such as the Asian king cobra and monitor lizards, eat their own kind. But reptiles' greatest enemies are humans. Crocodiles, snakes, and lizards are killed for their skins or because they are so feared; or captured so their venom can be used for medical research.

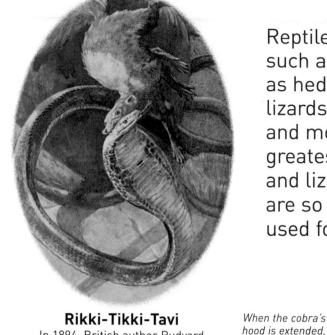

Rikki-Tikki-Tavi

In 1894, British author Rudyard Kipling wrote *The Jungle Book*, and created a hero in a little mongoose, Rikki-Tikki-Tavi. This mammal became the protector of a British family in India, first killing a lethal krait snake, and then a cobra (above). The cobra's strength is of little use to it once the mongoose has grasped the back of the snake's head.

When the cobra's hood is extended, the "eye" is meant to terrify aggressors

Enemy number one

One of the most famous enemies of many snakes, particularly of the cobra (left), is the mongoose (top right). In any fight, the mongoose is likely to win, relying on its speed and agility to avoid the snake's lunges. The mongoose will dart in and bite the back of the snake's neck, or it may grab the back of the snake's head until the snake gives up the struggle. Mongooses were introduced into the West Indies to reduce snake numbers, but became worse pests themselves, attacking small animals and poultry.

The cobra's body is bunched, ready for attack

Cobra

Hood spread in attack

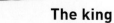

The king

Lions prey on crocodiles. On land, the lion's speed and power will overcome the more sluggish reptile. It might be a different story, though, in or near water.

Stiff hairs on the back of the mongoose are raised as added protection

Mongoose

Razor-sharp teeth bite the cobra behind the head

Body is lightly poised on back paws for quick movement

Feet first

The secretary bird (above) stamps its feet and flaps its wings to disturb prey. When a snake shows itself, the bird kicks or stamps on it, while covering the snake with its wings to keep it from moving into a position to defend itself. If stamping does not work, then the bird carries the snake high into the air and drops it.

War dance

In Indian mythology, demon Kaliya changed into a cobra and killed herdsmen in his search for the god Krishna. Krishna killed Kaliya, then danced on his head (above).

Tarzan triumphs!

Tarzan, the jungle hero (below), has no difficulty overpowering his reptilian enemy. In real life, a struggle between a crocodile and a human could have a very different ending. Crocodiles are not usually man-eaters, but they might attack someone foolish enough to stray near crocodile-infested rivers.

Just good friends

Shearwater

A helping hand

New Zealand's tuatara (right) live alongside seabirds such as petrels and shearwaters (above), and sometimes share their burrows. The birds cover the area in droppings. This attracts insects, including beetles and crickets—the tuatara's favorite food—but tuatara will also eat the nestling birds.

Because the majority of reptiles are meat-eaters, the relationship between them and other animals is usually that of predator and prey. However, a number of reptiles live with other animals in peace. Lizards and snakes, for example, will use the same termite mound to incubate their eggs. Tortoises and lizards have been known to share a burrow with opossums, racoons, rabbits, and rats. Even rattlesnakes can live peacefully with others in such a home.

Tuatara

A friend indeed

African helmeted turtles clean tiny parasites from hippopotamuses and rhinoceroses. Some turtles pull algae from other turtles' shells using their jaws—and then swap places.

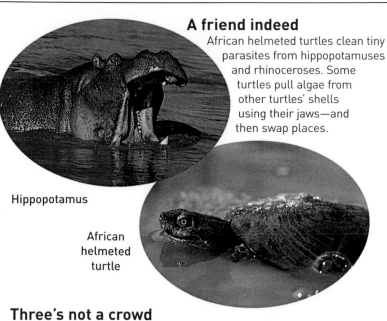

Hippopotamus

African helmeted turtle

Three's not a crowd

All sorts of reptiles end up living side by side, for different reasons. The hinge-back tortoise hides in its burrow from the hot African sun, waiting for rain. The house snake searches the same hole for rats and mice to eat, while the skink may be hiding from a predator.

Sleeping partners

Birds are sometimes said to pluck scraps of food and parasites from the gaping mouths of crocodiles (above). There is some doubt whether birds such as plovers would risk this, but some do safely wander among sleeping crocodiles. Some birds, such as the water dikkop, nest near crocodiles to the benefit of both; few animals will attack the birds with crocodiles nearby, and the birds' reaction to an enemy also warns the fearsome reptiles.

Cleaning up

Many animals outside the reptile world live in such a way that helping others means that they also help themselves. These small cleaner fish (above) are picking unwanted parasites from the large fish's skin. And, at the same time, they're getting a meal of food fragments that cling to the bigger fish.

An eye to the future

Unless we change our impact on the world, many reptiles may face extinction. Over 150 million years, the wide variety of reptiles has declined to just four groups, and they now face a greater threat than ever before—destruction by humans of the habitats to which they have become specially adapted. Today, governments are more aware, and are helping some species. Is it too little, too late?

Snakeskin wallets

Safe—for how long?
Although still fairly common, the giant skink of the Solomon Islands (above) faces a problem shared by many other reptiles—its habitat is rapidly being taken over by humans, and there is concern that these lizards will soon face extinction with the decline of their home and food source. This large skink has further problems—it is a common food for some people.

Beautiful soup
In some areas, reptiles are a popular food for humans. In the Caribbean, 5,000 marine turtles were turned into soup by just one food firm.

Tourist trap
Building for tourism has caused the loss of many of the loggerhead turtles' nesting sites in Turkey. This beautiful beach is one of the last remaining sites.

Baby big-headed turtle

Big head
The head of this well-named big-headed turtle (above) is so large that it cannot be drawn into its shell. Due to its strange appearance, it is often captured for the pet trade or used to make souvenirs. It lives in Southeast Asia, where it spends its days buried in gravel or under rocks in cool mountain streams.

An old engraving shows the large head

Siamese crocodile head keyring

Rattlesnake boot

Dirty dealing

In some countries, conservationists are trying to save reptiles. However, many are still being slaughtered to provide skins for the leather trade and souvenirs for tourists. Thousands of other reptiles are collected by the pet trade, although successful captive breeding has helped maintain some rare reptile species.

Unhappy pet

The Pacific Island boa (below) lives in a variety of habitats—forests, farms, and near human dwellings—on the Solomon Islands. The main danger to its existence is loss of habitat. It is chiefly a ground snake, but it climbs trees to feed on rodents, birds, and young lizards. It is sometimes kept as a pet, but often "sulks" in captivity, refusing to eat.

Down the ladder

Snakes are probably disappearing faster than any other vertebrate. Today, they are constantly in danger of being run over by cars. If something is not done to help them, we may be left with only games and models of these animals.

Bead snake made by prisoners of war in 1916

Reptile classification

About 9,400 types of reptile are known, and more are discovered each year. Like all living things, every type—or species—is classified, and given a two-part scientific name. Reptiles are an animal class that is divided into four orders—turtles and tortoises, crocodilians, tuatara, and snakes and lizards.

Upper and lower eyelids are joined to form turretlike eyes

Long, prehensile tail

Jackson's chameleon, *Trioceros jacksonii*

Extensible tongue is many times the length of its jaw

Sticky, club-shaped tip traps insects

Classifying reptiles

Jackson's chameleon, from East Africa, is also known as the three-horned chameleon, and has many other common names, too. Its scientific name, given by zoologist George Boulanger in 1896, is *Trioceros jacksonii*. Its body is flattened, it has feet divided into two groups of toes, it has a long, prehensile tail, and its eyes are housed in movable, turret-shaped structures. These features point to the fact that it belongs to the chameleon family—a distinctive group of reptiles.

Saddle-shaped markings on back

Dark stripe behind each eye

Boa, *Boa Constrictor*, coiled on a branch

Classification levels

In scientific classification, species are arranged in groups of increasing size. The boa constrictor is classified as the species *Boa constrictor*. This is one of four species in the genus *Boa*, which is in the family Boidae and includes 40 species of non-venomous snakes. Boidae is in the suborder Serpentes (which contains all snakes) and is part of the order Squamata (which contains snakes and lizards). Squamata is in the class Reptilia, which is in the phylum Chordata (and includes all animals with backbones).

Color varies across different parts of the snake

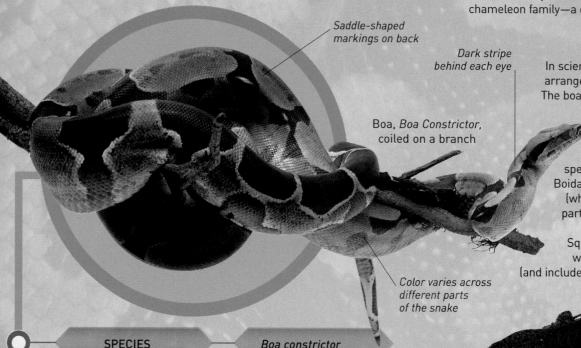

SPECIES	Boa constrictor
GENUS	Boa
FAMILY	Boidae
SUBORDER	Serpentes
ORDER	Squamata
CLASS	Reptilia
PHYLUM	Chordata

Dwarf gecko, *Sphaerodactylus ariasae*

New discoveries

Every year, new reptiles are discovered as scientists probe remote habitats and reexamine known species. Recent discoveries include one of the smallest of all reptiles—the dwarf gecko Jaragua sphaero (*Sphaerodactylus ariasae*), described in 2001. Also, Australia's Central Ranges taipan (*Oxyuranus temporalis*), identified in 2007 as one of the most venomous snakes in the world.

Turtles and tortoises

Reptiles in this order have a hard or rubbery shell enclosing soft parts of the body. They live on land as well as in water, and cut up their food with sharp-edged jaws.

Order: Testudines

Families: 13

Species: 317

Spotted turtle,
Clemmys guttata

Tuatara

Found only in New Zealand, tuatara resemble lizards but have a different skull structure and quite different ancestry. They grow slowly, but can live to a great age.

Order: Rhynchocephalia

Families: 1

Species: 2

Tuatara,
Sphenodon punctatus

Crocodilians

Semiaquatic predators, crocodilians have long bodies, powerful jaws, and eyes and nostrils positioned high on their heads. Their backs are protected by large, bony scales.

Order: Crocodylia

Families: 3

Species: 24

Nile crocodile,
Crocodylus niloticus

Snakes and lizards

Order: Squamata

Suborders: 3

Snakes

These legless predators have cylindrical bodies and gaping jaws. Some kill by constricting their prey; others bite with venomous fangs.

Suborder: Serpentes

Families: 18

Species: 3,400

Egyptian cobra,
Naja haje

Lizards

The most varied group of reptiles, lizards typically have four well-developed legs, keen senses, and eat meat. Often fast-moving, some shed their tails if attacked.

Suborder: Lacertilia

Families: 24

Species: 5,500

Rainbow agama,
Agama agama

Amphisbaenians

This group contains wormlike reptiles with cylindrical bodies and rings of scales. Shaped for life underground, they are rarely seen on the surface except after rain.

Suborder: Amphisbaena

Families: 6

Species: 181

Florida worm lizard,
Rhineura floridana

Reptile evolution

Reptiles first appeared on Earth more than 300 MYA, in the Carboniferous Period. They evolved into distinct groups and, by the Jurassic Period, they were the world's dominant animals—until an asteroid impact 65 MYA wiped out the non-bird dinosaurs and many other reptiles. Today, five evolutionary lines remain, including the direct descendants of dinosaurs—birds.

Skeleton of Edmontosaurus

Evidence from the past

Fossils play a key part in showing how reptiles have evolved. This skeleton (right) belongs to Edmontosaurus, a duck-billed ornithischian ("bird-hipped") dinosaur. It lived in the late Cretaceous Period, dying out when the asteroid hit Earth.

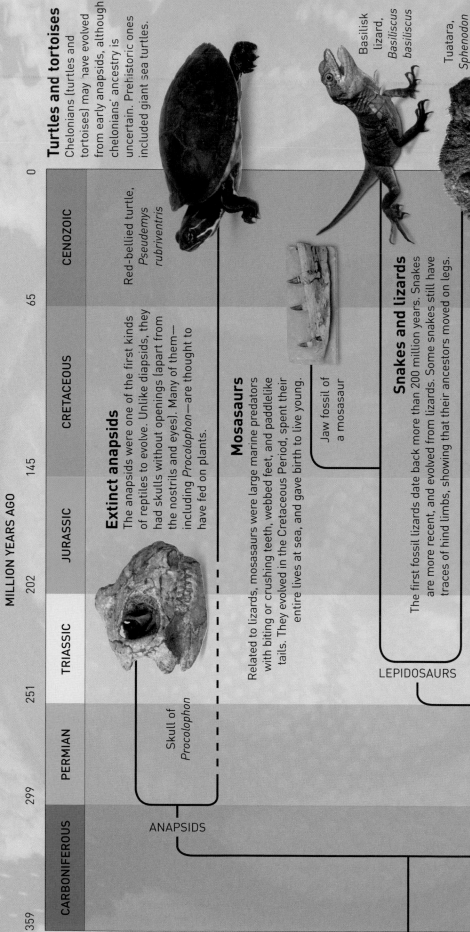

CARBONIFEROUS	PERMIAN	TRIASSIC	JURASSIC	CRETACEOUS	CENOZOIC
359	299	251	202	145	65	0

MILLION YEARS AGO

Extinct anapsids

The anapsids were one of the first kinds of reptiles to evolve. Unlike diapsids, they had skulls without openings (apart from the nostrils and eyes). Many of them—including Procolophon—are thought to have fed on plants.

Skull of *Procolophon*

ANAPSIDS

Turtles and tortoises

Chelonians (turtles and tortoises) may have evolved from early anapsids, although chelonians' ancestry is uncertain. Prehistoric ones included giant sea turtles.

Red-bellied turtle, *Pseudemys rubriventris*

Mosasaurs

Related to lizards, mosasaurs were large marine predators with biting or crushing teeth, webbed feet, and paddlelike tails. They evolved in the Cretaceous Period, spent their entire lives at sea, and gave birth to live young.

Jaw fossil of a mosasaur

Snakes and lizards

The first fossil lizards date back more than 200 million years. Snakes are more recent, and evolved from lizards. Some snakes still have traces of hind limbs, showing that their ancestors moved on legs.

Basilisk lizard, *Basiliscus basiliscus*

Tuatara, *Sphenodon punctatus*

LEPIDOSAURS

REPTILE EVOLUTION

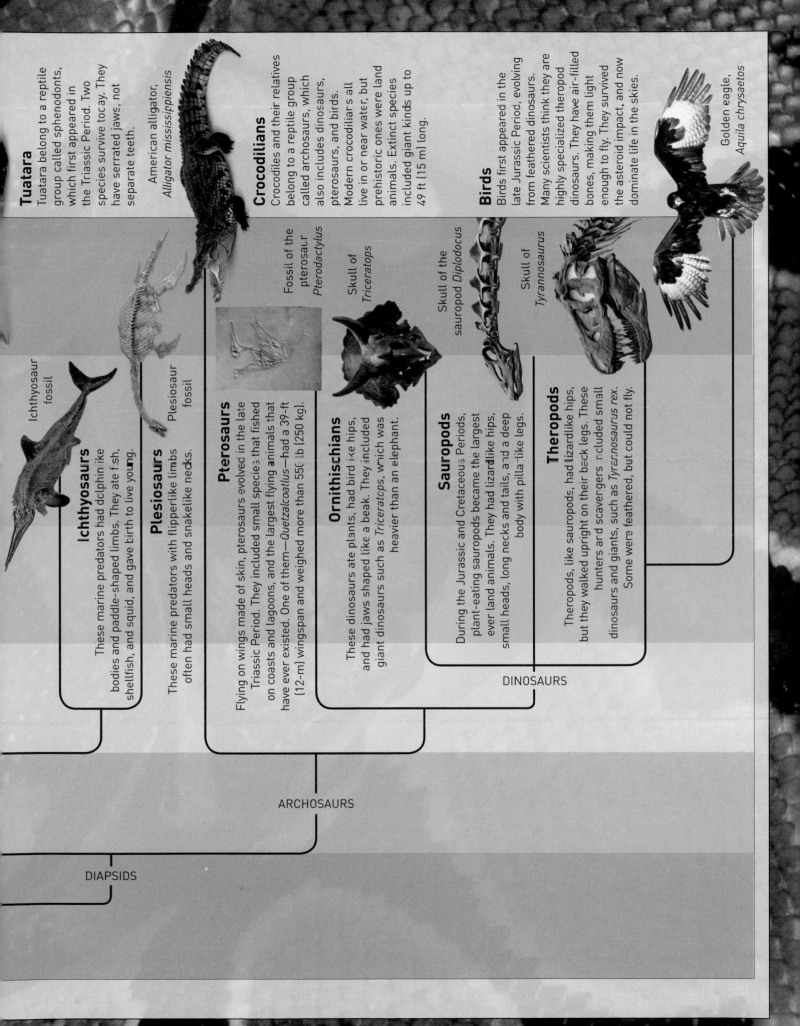

Tuatara

Tuatara belong to a reptile group called sphenodonts, which first appeared in the Triassic Period. Two species survive today. They have serrated jaws, not separate teeth.

American alligator, *Alligator mississippiensis*

Crocodilians

Crocodiles and their relatives belong to a reptile group called archosaurs, which also includes dinosaurs, pterosaurs, and birds. Modern crocodilians all live in or near water, but prehistoric ones were land animals. Extinct species included giant kinds up to 49 ft (15 m) long.

Birds

Birds first appeared in the late Jurassic Period, evolving from feathered dinosaurs. Many scientists think they are highly specialized theropod dinosaurs. They have air-filled bones, making them light enough to fly. They survived the asteroid impact, and now dominate life in the skies.

Golden eagle, *Aquila chrysaetos*

Ichthyosaur fossil

Fossil of the pterosaur *Pterodactylus*

Plesiosaur fossil

Skull of *Triceratops*

Skull of the sauropod *Diplodocus*

Skull of *Tyrannosaurus*

Ichthyosaurs

These marine predators had dolphin-like bodies and paddle-shaped limbs. They ate fish, shellfish, and squid, and gave birth to live young.

Plesiosaurs

These marine predators with flipperlike limbs often had small heads and snakelike necks.

Pterosaurs

Flying on wings made of skin, pterosaurs evolved in the late Triassic Period. They included small species that fished on coasts and lagoons, and the largest flying animals that have ever existed. One of them—*Quetzalcoatlus*—had a 39-ft (12-m) wingspan and weighed more than 550 lb (250 kg).

Ornithischians

These dinosaurs ate plants, had bird-like hips, and had jaws shaped like a beak. They included giant dinosaurs such as *Triceratops*, which was heavier than an elephant.

Sauropods

During the Jurassic and Cretaceous Periods, plant-eating sauropods became the largest ever land animals. They had lizardlike hips, small heads, long necks and tails, and a deep body with pillar-like legs.

Theropods

Theropods, like sauropods, had lizardlike hips, but they walked upright on their back legs. These hunters and scavengers included small dinosaurs and giants, such as *Tyrannosaurus rex*. Some were feathered, but could not fly.

DINOSAURS

ARCHOSAURS

DIAPSIDS

67

Threats

Nearly 10 percent of reptiles are endangered, or vulnerable to extinction in this century. Reptiles face many threats, including hunting and habitat change—especially harmful on islands where reptiles have nowhere else to go.

North America

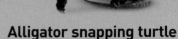

Wood turtle

Species: *Clemmys insculpta*

Status: Endangered

Suffers from road traffic and habitat change.

Alligator snapping turtle

Species: *Macrochelys temminckii*

Status: Vulnerable

Threats include drainage of its watery habitat, hunted for meat.

Central America and the Caribbean

Rhinoceros iguana

Species: *Cyclura cornuta*

Status: Vulnerable

Living only on the Caribbean island of Hispaniola, this iguana is threatened by deforestation, hunting, and attacks by feral animals, such as dogs and wild pigs.

American crocodile

Species: *Crocodylus acutus*

Status: Vulnerable

Hunted for food and its skin, and affected by water pollution.

South America

Galàpagos giant tortoise

Species: *Chelonoidis nigra*

Status: Vulnerable

This species is threatened by goats that were introduced to its island home and compete for its food.

Yellow-spotted river turtle

Species: *Podocnemis unifilis*

Status: Vulnerable

Vulnerable to hunting for its eggs and meat, and to capture for the pet trade.

Oceans

Leatherback Turtle

Species: *Dermochelys coriacea*

Status: Critically endangered

Threats include collisions with ships, fishing, and waste plastic, which it eats.

Arctic Ocean

North Pacific Ocean

NORTH AMERICA

North Atlantic Ocean

SOUTH AMERICA

South Pacific Ocean

South Atlantic Ocean

Europe

Spur-thighed tortoise

Species: *Testudo graeca*

Status: Vulnerable

Once collected for the pet trade, threats today include increased traffic and development.

Lilford's wall lizard

Species: *Podarcis lilfordi*

Status: Endangered

Found only in Spain's Balearic Islands, it is threatened by cats and other predators.

Asia

King cobra

Species: *Ophiophagus hannah*

Status: Vulnerable

This large, highly venomous snake is currently affected by deforestation, and by capture for food and use in traditional eastern medicine.

Yellow-margined box turtle

Species: *Cuora flavomarginata*

Status: Endangered

Found in ponds and rice paddies, this freshwater turtle is widely collected for food.

Arctic Ocean

Europe

Asia

North Pacific Ocean

Africa

Indian Ocean

Australia

Antarctica

Australasia and the Pacific

Brother's island tuatara

Species: *Sphenodon guntheri*

Status: Vulnerable

Vulnerable to attack by rats and other predators introduced to its island home from mainland New Zealand.

Fijian crested iguana

Species: *Brachylophus vitiensis*

Status: Critically endangered

Threats include deforestation and introduced goats, which destroy the iguana's habitat.

Ramsay's python

Species: *Aspidites ramsayi*

Status: Endangered

Threatened by grazing livestock, which destroy its habitat, and by introduced foxes.

Africa

Dwarf crocodile

Species: *Osteolaemus tetraspis*

Status: Vulnerable

This small crocodile is threatened by deforestation and by being hunted for food.

Armadillo lizard

Species: *Cordylus cataphractus*

Status: Vulnerable

Threats include the illegal pet trade—this slow-moving lizard is easy to collect.

Glossary

Body raised off the ground

Bipedal lizard running on hind legs

AMNION
A membrane that surrounds and protects a developing animal before it hatches or before it is born.

AMPHIBIAN
One of a group of cold-blooded vertebrates (backboned animals). They have moist skin and most lay eggs in water.

BASK
To warm up by lying in sunshine. Reptiles bask to raise their body temperature.

BINOCULAR VISION
Vision in which both eyes face forward, letting an animal see in 3-D. Humans have binocular vision.

BIPEDAL
Walking on two legs instead of four.

CARAPACE
The domed shell of a chelonian, made of hard scales, or scutes, over plates of bone.

CARNIVORE
Any animal that eats other animals.

CARTILAGE
A tough, flexible substance between bones, letting them slide over each other at joints.

CHELONIANS
Reptile group that includes tortoises and turtles, and has a bony or leathery shell.

CLASSIFICATION
A way of identifying living things and showing how they are linked through evolution.

CLUTCH
A group of eggs, laid at the same time.

COLD-BLOODED
An animal that uses the Sun's heat to keep warm. Most living reptiles are cold-blooded; only a few can keep warm by using energy from food.

CONSTRICTION
Suffocating prey by slowly squeezing it to death.

EGG TOOTH
A special "tooth" that young reptiles use to tear open their eggs from the inside. It usually goes after the animal's first molt.

EMBRYO
A young animal in the very early stages of development, before it is ready to hatch or be born.

EVOLUTION
Gradual changes in living things that build up over many generations, changing the way they look and the way they live. In reptiles, evolution has produced a huge range of different animals, although some are now extinct.

EXTINCTION
The permanent dying-out of a species of living things.

FANGS
In snakes, specialized teeth that inject venom. Most fangs are fixed in place, but some fold away when not in use.

FERTILIZATION
The moment when a male and female cell join to produce a new living thing. In reptiles, fertilization occurs before the female lays her eggs or gives birth.

FOSSIL
The remains of something that was once alive, buried and preserved in rock. Fossils provide evidence for reptiles that existed in the past, such as dinosaurs.

HABITAT
The surroundings that an animal normally lives in and that provide it with everything it needs to survive.

HEAT-SENSITIVE PITS
Special pits near some snakes' jaws that detect heat coming from warm-blooded prey.

ICHTHYOSAURS
Extinct marine reptiles with streamlined bodies, four flippers, and a fishlike tail.

INCUBATION
The period when a young animal develops inside an egg. Most reptile eggs are kept warm by their surroundings; a few are warmed by the mother.

INNER EAR
Part of the ear that is hidden inside the skull. It collects sound vibrations and converts them into signals for the brain.

JACOBSON'S ORGAN
A special organ located in the roof of the mouth of reptiles and other animals wih backbones. Most snakes flick it in and out to "taste" scents.

KERATIN
A tough substance that gives reptile scales their strength. Keratin is also found in mammals' hooves and hair.

LEAF LITTER
A layer of dead leaves on the ground, often full of small animals. It is an important habitat for some lizards and snakes.

LIGAMENT
A band of cartilage that holds bones together at joints. Snake jaws have

Fossil skull of *Cynognathus*, a mammal-like reptile

unusually elastic ligaments, which lets them stretch wide when swallowing prey.

LIVING FOSSIL
A species that has changed very little over millions of years. Tuatara are examples of living fossils.

MELANOPHORES
Special cells in a reptile's skin that contain chemical colors, or pigments. By moving the pigments, the cells can change the skin's overall color and patterning.

METABOLIC RATE
The speed at which an animal converts food into energy. In reptiles, metabolic rate is affected by outside warmth—the warmer it is, the faster their bodies work. In cold weather, reptiles often become inactive, because their metabolic rate drops to a low level.

MOLTING
Shedding the outer skin layer. Most reptiles molt throughout their lives.

MONITOR LIZARDS
A family of lizards that includes the

Carapace

world's largest species, the Komodo dragon. All have heavy bodies, large claws, and long, forked tongues.

NOCTURNAL
Active after dark. Tropical reptiles are often nocturnal, because nights are warm enough for them to stay active.

PARASITE
An animal that lives on or inside another and uses it as its food.

PARENTAL CARE
Caring for the young after they have hatched, or after they have been born. Parental care is rare in reptiles, except among crocodiles and their relatives.

PARTHENOGENESIS
Producing young without mating.

PLASTRON
The lower part of a chelonian's shell. Unlike the upper part (carapace), the plastron is usually flat; it may be hinged so that the animal can seal its head inside.

PLESIOSAURS
Extinct marine reptiles with flipper-shaped limbs and, often, a long neck.

PREDATOR
An animal that hunts others to eat. Most reptiles are predators, feeding on a range of animals from insects to mammals and birds. Some kinds—particularly snakes—specialize in eating other reptiles.

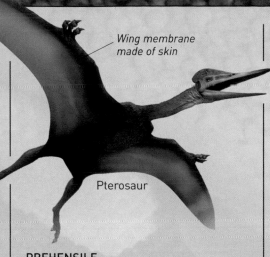

Wing membrane made of skin

Pterosaur

PREHENSILE
Able to curl around and grip. Tree snakes and chameleons have prehensile tails.

PREY
Any animal that is food for a predator.

PTEROSAURS
Extinct flying reptiles with long wings.

RECTILINEAR MOTION
A way of moving—used by some snakes—with the body kept in a straight line; snakes use groups of belly scales as anchors while others lift off the ground.

SCALES
The hard plates covering the outside of a reptile's body, made of keratin and joined by bands of flexible skin.

SCUTE
A scale that is reinforced by bone, such as on crocodiles' bodies.

TERRITORY
The area claimed by an animal (usually the male) to feed and breed in.

ULTRASOUNDS
Sounds that are too high-pitched for human ears to hear.

VENOM
Poisons produced by snakes and other animals, used in self-defense or for killing prey. Snake venom usually includes a range of substances, such as nerve poisons and anticoagulants that produce internal bleeding.

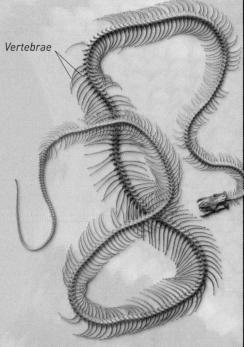

Vertebrae

VERTEBRA (plural: VERTEBRAE)
The individual bones that make up the backbone, or spine.

VERTEBRATE
Any animal that has a backbone. Vertebrates include fish, amphibians, reptiles, birds, and mammals.

VESTIGIAL LIMB
A leg that has evolved into a very small size and no longer works for moving.

VIVIPAROUS
Giving birth to live young.

WARM-BLOODED
An animal that uses energy from food to keep its body warm. Unlike reptiles, they stay warm all the time and so can stay active, whatever the temperature.

WEBBED FEET
Feet with toes that are joined together by skin flaps, often found in water-dwelling reptiles.

YOLK
A store of food inside an egg, which lets a young animal develop.

Monitor lizard

Forked tongue

SERUM
A substance used to counter the effects of a snakebite. Serum, or antivenom, is made by collecting snake venom.

SIDEWINDING
A way of moving used by snakes crossing open sand; the snake repeatedly throws its body diagonally through the air, leaving a series of J-shaped tracks.

SPECIES
The most important level in the classification of living things. Members of a species look like each other, and can breed to produce fertile young.

Index

Acknowledgments

Dorling Kindersley would like to thank: Trevor Smith and all the staff at Trevor Smith's Animal World for their help and enthusiasm. Cyril Walker at the Natural History Museum for pages 8 and 9. Keith Brown, Isolde McGeorge and Chester Zoo for their kind permission to photograph tuatara. **Proofreading:** Caitlin Doyle; **Index:** Helen Peters. Niki Foreman for editing the relaunch version and Polly Goodman for proofreading it.

The publisher would like to thank the following for their kind permission to reproduce their photographs:

Picture Credits
(Key: a-above; b-below/bottom; c-center; f-far; l-left; r-right; t-top)

A.N.T./P & M Walton/N.H.P.A.: 10br; 56tl
Ancient Art & Achitecture Collection: 34b

Aquila Photographics: 60tl
Ardea: /J.A. Bailey 22tr; /Jean-Paul Ferrero 48br
E.N. Arnold: 14bl
Biofotos/S.Summerhays: 23br **Bridgeman Art Library:** 26b; 62ml **British Museum (Natural History):** 9m, **Jane Burton** 25b © **Casterman:** 40tr
Bruce Coleman Ltd: 33mr; /M. Fogden 7mr; /A. Stevens 7b, 42tr, 53br; /P. Davey 14mr, 38ml; /F. Lauting 19tr; / E. Bauer 19m; /D. Hughes 21b; /J. & D. Bartlett 28l; /C. Ott 33br; /J. Burton 38tl; /G. Zeisler 41ml; /B. Wood 42m; / J. Foote 42bc, 62tl; /R. Williams 46bm; /L. Lee Rue III 56tr; /M. Brulton 62–63t; / C. Frith 62t
Corbis: James L. Amos 69cr, S. Blair Hedges / epa 64br, Martin Harvey 68bc, Joe McDonald 70tc, Gary Meszaros / Visuals Unlimited 68cl, Michael & Patricia Fogden 69fbr, David A. Northcott 68bl; **Dorling Kindersley:** 24m; Lars Bergendorf

69tc, Hunterian Museum (University of Glasgow) 67cl, Natural History Museum, London 66cr, 66cb, 67c, 67fcl, 70cr, 71cr; Jerry Young – DK Images 67tl, 69bl;
Mary Evans Picture Library: 7tr; 8tl; 17tl; 18tl; 27tr; 38mr; 40mr; 43tl; 50–51; 57tm; 58tl
Sally & Richard Greenhill: 24mr
Robert Harding Picture Library: 14br; 16t; 47tl; 57mr
Michael Holford: 30tl; 34tr
Kobal Collection: 43tm
Frank Lane Picture Agency: 60m
Getty Images: Rod Patterson / Gallo Images 69br, Dea Picture Library / De Agostini Picture Library 69tl, Patricio Robles Gil / age fotostock 69crb; **Musee National d'Histoire Naturelle, Paris:** 30ml
National Museum of Wales: 30mr
N.H.P.A.: 57ml; 61tm
Natural Science Photos: /P.H. & S.L. Ward 32
Oxford Scientific Films: 52tl; 61tl; /S. Osolinski 18m; /K. Atkinson 37br; /Z. Leszczynski 41mr, 46bl; /J. Gerlach 42bl; / Stouffer Productions 54m; /S. Mills 62br
Photoshot: Bill Love 65br;

Planet Earth Pictures: 61br; /K. Lucas 20m; /P. Scoones 37tr
Ann Ronan Picture Library: 22bm **South Kensington Antiques:** 62bc **Frank Spooner Pictures:** 28br **Syndication International:** 6ml
By Courtesy of the Board of Trustees of the Victoria & Albert Museum: 34m
Wildlight Photo Agency/Oliver Strewe: 21tr
Jerry Young: 42c, 43c, 67tl, 69bl
Illustrations by Andrew Macdonald: 13; 17; 21; 38; 41; 42; 47; 51; 53

All other images © Dorling Kindersley

For further information, see:
www.dkimages.com